MUSIC ACCOMPANIMENT
FOR THE
FUNERAL MASS

THE ORDER OF CHRISTIAN FUNERALS

MUSIC ACCOMPANIMENT
FOR THE
FUNERAL MASS

THE LITURGICAL PRESS

Collegeville, Minnesota

Nihil obstat: Rev. Robert C. Harren, J.C.L., *Censor deputatus.*
Imprimatur: ✚ Jerome Hanus, O.S.B., Bishop of St. Cloud. August 16, 1989.

Introduction

The *Funeral Mass—People's Booklet* and this accompaniment have been designed for use both in parishes with fuller music ministries and in smaller parishes with limited musical resources. Musical selections reflecting various levels of musical difficulty have been included so that those with abundant resources "may have something to yearn for" and those whose musical fare is necessarily simpler "may have nothing to run from" (*Rule of Benedict*, ch. 64).

"Music is integral to the funeral rites. It allows the community to express convictions and feelings that words alone may fail to convey. It has the power to console and uplift the mourners and to strengthen the unity of the assembly in faith and love" (General Introduction, *Order of Christian Funerals*, no. 30). Of first importance is the musical participation of the assembly itself, for the healing and hope-filled presence of Christ is powerfully and vividly experienced in the sung prayer of the worshiping assembly. In addition, the full range of parish music ministries—cantors/song leaders, instrumentalists, choirs—should be used to support the sung prayer of the assembly.

Many of the musical selections in this collection may be used regularly at Sunday Eucharist (taking care to respect copyrighted material). We encourage parishes to experience the rich variety of music within this collection by expanding the parish repertoire. In this way, much of the music used at funerals may become well known by the parishioners. For example, some parishes may wish to prepare seasonal song leaflets in which music from this collection may be introduced to the larger parish repertoire; also, a demonstration tape available from The Liturgical Press may assist the choir or parish to learn new pieces.

Some of the psalms used here are "Common Texts for Sung Responsorial Psalms," that is, they may be sung throughout the Liturgical Year in place of the printed Sunday responsorial psalm (see *General Instruction of the Roman Missal*, no. 36; *Lectionary*, no. 175). For example, Psalm 25 may be sung for the whole season of Advent; Psalms 27, 63, and 103 may be used during Ordinary Time for a few weeks; Psalm 42 might be used during some weeks of Lent, etc.

"Many parishes have found it helpful to form choirs of retired parishioners or others who are at home on weekdays, whose unique ministry it is to assist the grieving members of a funeral assembly by leading the sung prayer of the funeral liturgy" (*Liturgical Music Today*, NCCB, 1982, no. 32). We encourage the development of a funeral choir to enliven and support the participation of the assembly. If this cannot be done, a cantor/song leader should be used to perform a similar ministry. "In all cases a serious effort should be made to move beyond the practice of employing a 'funeral singer' to perform all the sung parts of the liturgy" (*Liturgical Music Today*, no. 32).

Because it is difficult to teach a new hymn tune within the Funeral Liturgy itself, familiar alternate tunes are given immediately following a new melody (see, for example, nos. 75, 75A, and 75B). New tunes may also be sung by the choir at designated "choir" times, e.g., at the Preparation of the Gifts or at Communion. In some parishes, new tunes may be picked up by asking the choir to sing one or two verses of a new tune, then inviting the assembly to join in on the remaining verses.

The following suggestions are offered to derive full use of these books.

Responsorial Psalm

• After the first reading and the silence that follows, the People's Booklet lists six refrains that may be used. The *complete text and music* for these refrains are found at other numbers in the book (see the Index). Besides those six psalms, other psalms may be used as a responsorial psalm.

- If a cantor is not available to sing the verses of psalms, the refrain may still be sung, with the verses read.
- Responsorial-type music is also well suited for the Communion procession. Choir/cantor sings the verses, the assembly sings the refrain.

Acclamations During the Eucharistic Prayer

- To give a sense of unity to the Eucharistic Prayer, we strongly encourage the use of acclamations (i.e., Sanctus, Memorial Acclamation, ''Amen'') that are melodically related or that ''fit'' with one another. For example, if Vermulst's Sanctus (no. 15) is used, other pieces from the same Mass (Memorial Acclamation nos. 19, 22, 24, or 25; ''Amen'' no. 26) should also be used. These other acclamations are by the same composers:

Sanctus	Memorial Acclamation	''Amen''
16	20	27
17	23	28
18	21	29

Communion Rite

- The Lord's Prayer, if sung, should be sung by all.
- The ''Lamb of God'' is sung to the action of breaking the bread (and pouring the cup). Additional verses of some settings are provided to accompany the action. The final verse is always ''Lamb of God . . . grant us peace.''

Rite of Commendation

- The Song of Farewell should be sung. Any of the choices given (nos. 35–39) or another appropriate song may be used.

Procession to the Place of Committal

The song ''May the Angels'' is given in two forms: a responsorial version (no. 40) and a hymn setting (no. 41). One of these versions (or another suitable text) is to be sung during the procession to the entrance of the church.

Finally, a word about the convenient use of these books:

- If a hymn tune has been used in this book more than once, the accompaniment is given in alternate keys. The location of alternate keys (higher or lower) is noted in each case below the title.
- The song leader/choir may use the *Funeral Mass—People's Booklet*, since both melody and text are given therein.

Numbers 1 through 6 in the People's Booklet are refrains for use after the first reading. Accompaniment for them is found at the numbers listed below.

1   Accompaniment is found at number 57.

2   Accompaniment is found at number 47.

3   Accompaniment is found at number 50.

4   Accompaniment is found at number 54.

5   Accompaniment is found at number 45.

6   Accompaniment is found at number 49.

7 Alleluia

Al - le - lu - ia, al - le - lu - ia, al - le - lu - ia.

Chant, mode VI

8 Alleluia

Cantor
Al - le - lu - ia.
Congregation
Al - le - lu - ia.
Cantor
Al - le - lu - ia.

Organ

Congregation
Al - le - lu - ia.
Cantor
Al - le - lu - ia.
Congregation
Al - le - lu - ia.

Howard Hughes, s.m., copyright ©1973, G.I.A. Publications, Inc.

Alleluia

Al - le - lu - ia, al - le - lu -

ia, al - le - lu - ia!

Michael Marcotte, O.S.B., copyright ©1979, the Order of Saint Benedict, Inc.

10   Alleluia, Ye Sons and Daughters

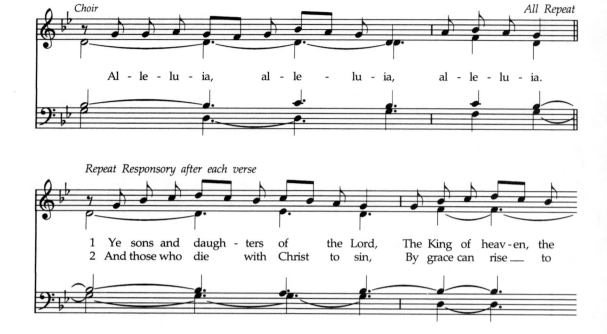

Choir ... *All Repeat*

Al - le - lu - ia, al - le - lu - ia, al - le - lu - ia.

Repeat Responsory after each verse

1 Ye sons and daugh - ters of the Lord, The King of heav - en, the
2 And those who die with Christ to sin, By grace can rise — to

King a - dored, From death to life has been re-stored. Al - le - lu - ia.
life a - gain, With him e - ter - nal vic - t'ry win. Al - le - lu - ia.

Text: J. Tisserand, 1494, English text by Irwin Udulutsch, o.f.m. cap., copyright ©1959, 1977, The Order of St. Benedict, Inc.
Tune: 15th century chant, mode II

Alleluia

INTRODUCTION

Fast; with driving power (♩. = 63)

REFRAIN

Al - le - lu - ia! Al - le - lu - ia! Al - le - lu - ia!

Alleluia, Praise and Glory 12

Cantor/Congr.

1 Al - le - lu - ia, _____ Al - le - lu - ia, _____
2 Praise and glo - ry, _____ Lord Je - sus Christ. _____

Al - le - lu - ia, _____ Al - le - lu - ia. _____
Praise and hon - or, _____ O word of God. _____

13   Glory and Praise to You

ANTIPHON *for equal or mixed voices*

Glo - ry and praise to you, Lord Je - sus Christ!

14   Praise to You

Cantor; All repeat

Praise to you, Lord Je - sus Christ, king of end - less glo - ry!

PSALM TONE FOR VERSE
Cantor/Choir

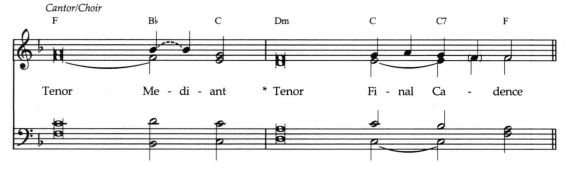

Tenor   Me - di - ant   * Tenor   Fi - nal Ca - dence

Sanctus

Holy, ho - ly, ho - ly Lord, God of pow-er and might,
heav - en and earth are full of your glo - ry. Ho -
san - na in the high - est. Bless - ed is he who
comes in the name of the Lord. Ho - san - na in the high - est.

Jan M. Vermulst, "A People's Mass," copyright ©1970, World Library Publications, Inc.

Sanctus

Ho - ly, ho - ly, ho - ly Lord, God of pow-er and might,

heav'n and earth are full of your glo - ry. Ho -

san - na in the high - est, ho - san - na in the high-est.

Blest is he who comes in the name of the Lord. Ho -

Richard Proulx, "A Community Mass," copyright ©1970, G.I.A. Publications, Inc.

Sanctus

Ho - ly, ho - ly, ho - ly Lord, God of power and might, heav - en and earth are full of your glo - ry. Ho - san - na in the high - est. Bless - ed is he who comes in the name of the Lord. Ho - san - na in the high - est.

Jonathan Tuuk, "Mass of the Holy Trinity," copyright ©1978, G.I.A. Publications, Inc.

Sanctus

19

Christ Has Died

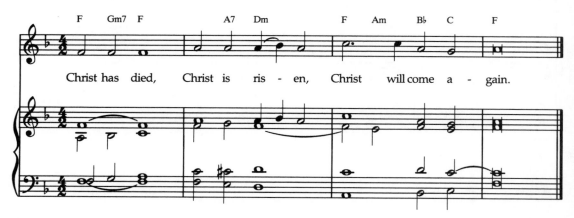

Christ has died, Christ is ris - en, Christ will come a - gain.

20

Christ Has Died

Christ has died, Christ is ris-en, Christ will come a - gain.

21

Christ Has Died

Christ has died, Christ is ris - en, Christ will come a - gain.

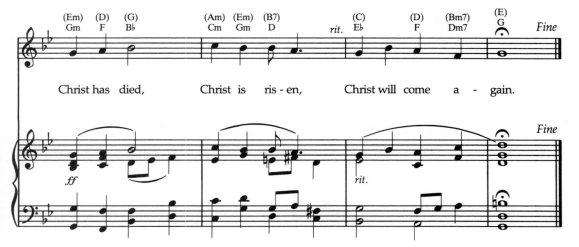

Christ has died, Christ is ris-en, Christ will come a-gain.

Marty Haugen, "Mass of Creation," copyright ©1984, G.I.A. Publications, Inc.

Dying You Destroyed Our Death   22

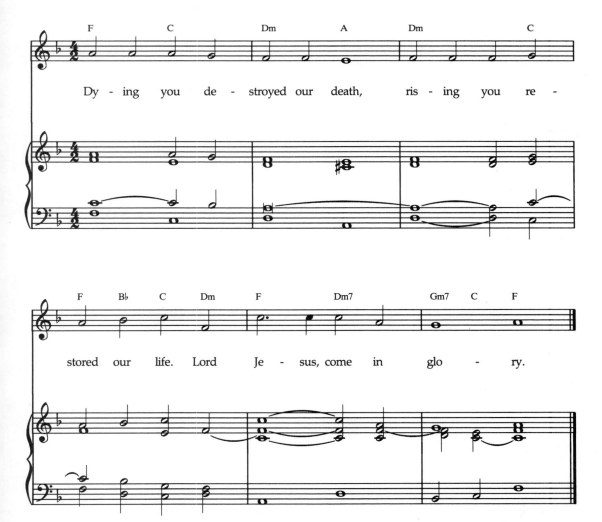

Dy-ing you de-stroyed our death, ris-ing you re-stored our life. Lord Je-sus, come in glo-ry.

Jan M. Vermulst, "A People's Mass," copyright ©1984, World Library Publications, Inc.

23 Dying You Destroyed Our Death

Dy - ing you de-stroyed our death, ris - ing you re-stored our life. Lord Je - sus, come in glo - ry.

Jonathan Tuuk, "Mass of the Holy Trinity," copyright ©1978, G.I.A. Publications, Inc.

24 When We Eat This Bread

When we eat this bread and drink this cup, we pro - claim your

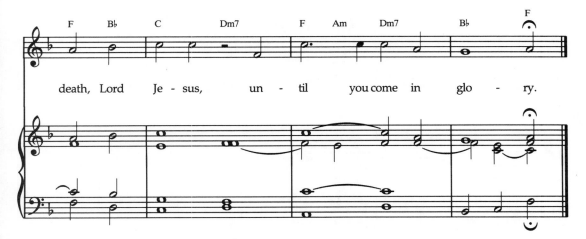

death, Lord Je - sus, un - til you come in glo - ry.

Lord, by Your Cross and Resurrection 25

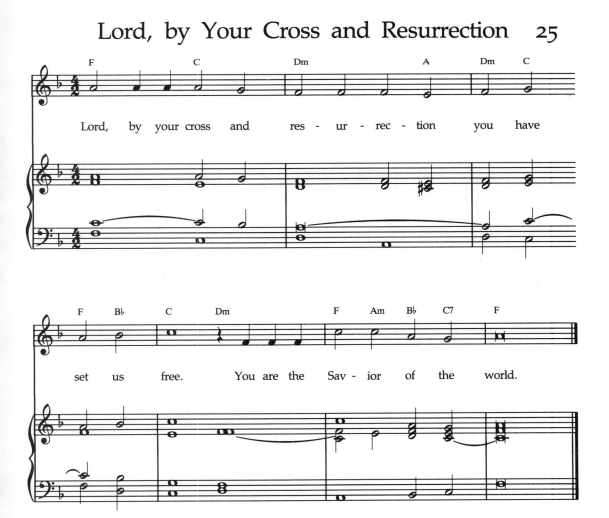

Lord, by your cross and res - ur - rec - tion you have

set us free. You are the Sav - ior of the world.

26

Great Amen

A - men, a - men, a - men.

27

Great Amen

A - men, a - men, al - le - lu - ia.

During Lent A - men, a - men, a - men.

(♩=c.72)

f (Reeds)

Ped.

Jonathan Tuuk, "Mass of the Holy Trinity," copyright ©1978, G.I.A. Publications, Inc.

Great Amen 29

Marty Haugen, "Mass of Creation," copyright ©1984, G.I.A. Publications, Inc.

Lamb of God

1 Lamb of God, you take a - way the sins of the
3 Lamb of God, true bread of life, the food of our

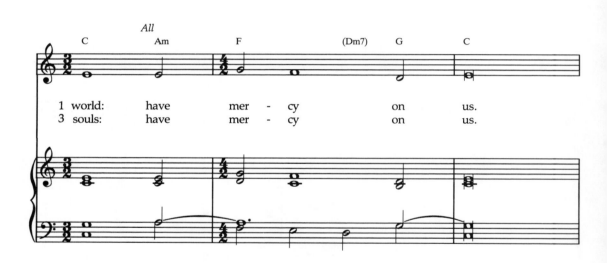

1 world: have mer - cy on us.
3 souls: have mer - cy on us.

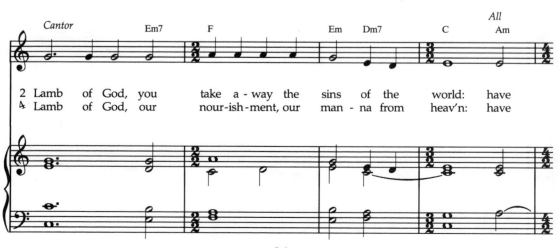

2 Lamb of God, you take a - way the sins of the world: have
4 Lamb of God, our nour-ish-ment, our man - na from heav'n: have

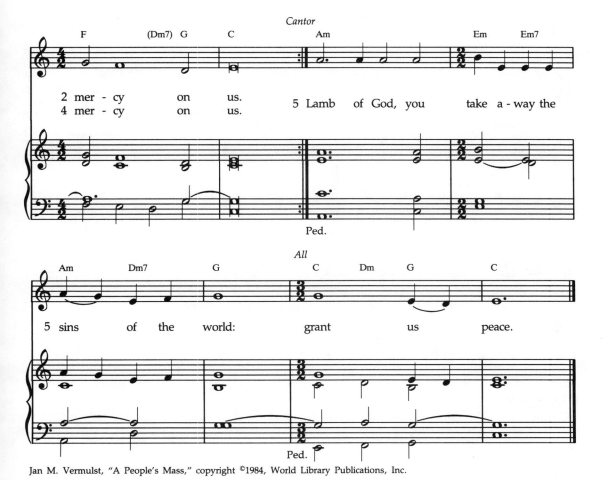

Lamb of God

Lamb of God

Lamb of God, you take a - way the sins of the world: have mer - cy on us.

Lamb of God, you take a - way the sins of the world:

grant us peace, grant us peace.

Becket Senchur, O.S.B., ''Trinity Mass,'' copyright ©1985, St. Vincent Archabbey, Latrobe, Pa.

Lamb of God

1 Lamb _____ of God,
2 Son _____ of God,
3 Christ _____ the Lord, you take a-way the sins of the world:

Last time:
Lamb _____ of God,

have mer - cy on us. grant us peace.

Additional Verses:

Word made flesh. . . Bread of life. . .
Paschal Lamb. . . Lord of love. . .

David Clark Isele, "Holy Cross Mass," copyright ©1979, G.I.A. Publications, Inc.

Jesus, Lamb of God

Capo 3

Cantor/Choir:
1 Je - sus, Lamb of God,
2 Je - sus, Bread of Life,
3 Je - sus, Prince of Peace,

All:
you take a - way the

sins of the world: have mer - cy on us.

FINAL TIME

Cantor/Choir: Je - sus, Lamb of

God, you take a-way the **sins** of the **world:** grant us your peace.

Additional Verses:

Jesus, Word of God. . .   Jesus, King of Kings. . .
Jesus, Tree of Life. . .   Jesus, Cup of Life. . .
Jesus, Ancient Cup. . .   Jesus, Fire of Love. . .
Jesus, Lord of Lords. . .   Jesus, Bread of Peace. . .
Jesus, Hope for all. . .

Marty Haugen, "Mass of Creation," copyright ©1984, G.I.A. Publications, Inc.

Come to His/Her Aid

(Song of Farewell)

35

1 Come to his* aid O saints of God; Come,
2 May Christ, who called you, take you home, And
3 Give him* e - ter - nal rest, O Lord. May
4 I know that my Re - deem - er lives; The

meet him,* an - gels of the Lord.
an - gels lead you_to A - bra - ham.
light un - end - ing shine on him.*
last day I shall rise a - gain.

Re - ceive his* soul, O ho - ly

ones; Pre - sent him* now to God, Most High.

*The pronoun is changed to fit gender and number.

Text: Dennis C. Smolarski, S.J., b. 1947, copyright ©1981, Dennis C. Smolarski, S.J.
    All rights reserved. Used with permission.
Tune: OLD HUNDREDTH, L.M., Louis Bourgeois, c. 1510–1561

36

Saints of God
(Song of Farewell)

Declamato (freely)

Cantor mp ($\d$=72)

Saints of God, come to her* aid! Come to meet her,* an-gels of the Lord!

All

Re - ceive her* soul(s) and pre - sent her* to God the Most

Cantor

High. May Christ, who called you, take you to him - self;

may an - gels lead you to A - bra - ham's side.

*The pronoun is changed to fit gender and number.

Text: *Rite of Funerals*, copyright ©1970, ICEL. All rights reserved.
Tune: SANCTI DEI, Irreg. with response, Phillip Duffy, from *Music for Rite of Funerals and Rite of Baptism for Children*, copyright ©1977, ICEL. All rights reserved.

Come to His/Her Aid

(Song of Farewell)

37

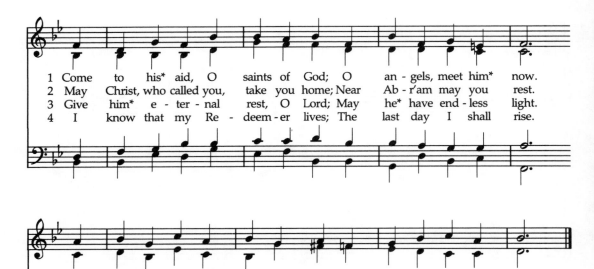

1 Come to his* aid, O saints of God; O an - gels, meet him* now.
2 May Christ, who called you, take you home; Near Ab - r'am may you rest.
3 Give him* e - ter - nal rest, O Lord; May he* have end - less light.
4 I know that my Re - deem - er lives; The last day I shall rise.

Re - ceive his* soul, pre - sent him* now to God, the Lord Most High.

*The pronoun is changed to fit gender and number.

Text: Dennis C. Smolarski, s.j., b. 1947, copyright ©1981, Dennis C. Smolarski, s.j.
    All rights reserved. Used with permission.
Tune: ST. ANNE, C.M., attr. to William Croft, 1678–1727

I Know That My Redeemer Lives

(Song of Farewell)

rise a-gain; in my bod-y I shall look on God, my Sav - ior,

in my bod-y I shall look on God, my Sav - ior.

I my-self shall see him; my own eyes will gaze on him,

my own eyes will gaze on him; ____ in my bod - y I shall

look on God, my Sav - ior, ____ in my bod - y I shall

look on God, my Sav - ior. ____ This is the hope I cher - ish,

41

this is the hope I cher-ish in my heart; _____ in my

bod-y I shall look on God, my Sav-ior, _____ in my

bod-y I shall look on God, my Sav-ior. _____

I Know That My Redeemer Lives

(Song of Farewell)

1 I know that my Re - deem - er lives! What joy the
2 He lives tri - um - phant from the grave; He lives e -
3 He lives to grant me rich sup - ply; He lives to
4 He lives to si - lence all my fears; He lives to

blest as - sur - ance gives! He lives, he lives, who
ter - nal - ly to save; He lives in maj - es -
guide me with his eye; He lives to com - fort
wipe a - way my tears; He lives to calm my

once was dead; He lives, my ev - er - liv - ing head!
ty a - bove; He lives to guide his Church in love.
me when faint; He lives to hear my soul's com - plaint.
trou - bled heart; He lives all bless - ings to im - part.

5 He lives to bless me with his love;
He lives to plead for me above;
He lives my hungry soul to feed;
He lives to help in time of need.

6 He lives, my kind, wise, heav'nly friend;
He lives and loves me to the end;
He lives, and while he lives, I'll sing;
He lives, my Prophet, Priest, and King!

7 He lives and grants me daily breath;
He lives, and I shall conquer death;
He lives my mansion to prepare;
He lives to bring me safely there.

8 He lives, all glory to his name!
He lives, my Savior, still the same;
What joy this blest assurance gives:
I know that my Redeemer lives!

Text: Based on Job 19:25; Samuel Medley, 1738–1799
Tune: DUKE STREET, L.M., attr. to John Hatton, c. 1710–1793

May the Angels

may the mar-tyrs come to wel-come you and take you to the ho - ly

cit - y, the new and e-ter-nal Je - ru-sa-lem.

Cantor or Choir

May the choir of an - gels wel-come you Where Laz-a-rus is poor no

long - er, may you have e - ter - nal rest,

may you have e - ter - nal rest.

(If concluding here, use this ending.)

May the an - gels lead you in - to par - a - dise;

May the an - gels lead you in - to par - a - dise;

may the mar - tyrs come to wel - come you and

may the mar - tyrs come to wel - come you

take you to the ho-ly cit-y, the new and e-ter-nal Je-ru-sa-lem. May you have e-ter-nal rest.

and take you to the ho-ly cit-y, the new and e-ter-nal Je-ru-sa-lem. May you have e-ter-nal rest.

May you have e-ter-nal rest.

May you have e-ter-nal rest.

opt. div.

molto rit.

long

Text: From the *Rite of Funerals*, copyright ©1970, ICEL
Tune: MAY THE ANGELS, Irreg., Howard Hughes, s.m.,
    from *Music for Rite of Funerals and Rite of Baptism for Children*, copyright ©1977, ICEL

41   May Flights of Angels

May flights of an-gels lead you on your way To par-a-dise, and heav'ns e-ter-nal day! May mar-tyrs greet you af-ter death's dark night, And bid you en-ter in-to Si-on's light! May choirs of an-gels sing you to your rest With once poor Laz-'rus, now for-ev-er blest!

Text: *In paradisum*, tr. James Quinn, s.j., copyright ©1969 by James Quinn, s.j.
   Reprinted by permission of Geoffrey Chapman (a division of Cassell, Ltd.), 1 Vincent Square, London SW1P, 2PN
Tune: William Henry Monk, 1823–1889

Be Not Afraid

I speak your words in* for-eign lands and all will un - der - stand.

1 You shall see the face of God and live. _____ *(Antiphon)*

ANTIPHON

Be not a - fraid. I go be - fore you al - ways.

Come fol-low Me, and I will give you rest.

*In the first edition of *Glory and Praise*, this phrase appeared as "to foreign men and they."

2 know that I am with you through it all. _____ (Antiphon)

VERSE 3 with Descant

3 Bless-ed are your poor, for the King-dom shall be theirs.

3 Blest are you that weep and mourn, for one day you shall laugh. And if

3 wick-ed men in-sult and hate you all be-cause of Me,

3 bless-ed, bless-ed are you! _____

ANTIPHON

Be not a-fraid. I go be-fore you al-ways.

Come fol-low Me, and I will give you

rest. _____

Fine

43 Blest Are They

INTRODUCTION

Tenderly, prayerfully (♩=ca. 112-120)

VERSE 1

1 Blest are they, the poor in spir - it, theirs is the

1 king-dom of God. _____ Blest are they full of

1 sor - row, they shall be con - soled. _____ Re -

REFRAIN

VERSE 4

Men: *mf* (Gsus) (G) (D/F#) (C)

4 Blest are they who seek peace; they are the

4 chil-dren of God. _____ Blest are they who

(to refrain, then verse 5)

4 suf-fer in faith, the glo-ry of God is theirs. _____ Re -

VERSE 5

Solo: (Gsus) (G) (D/F#) (C)

5 Blest are you who suf - fer hate, all be -

58

Words: The Beatitudes, Mt. 5:3–12; David Haas
Music: David Haas; vocal arr. David Haas and Michael Joncas
Copyright ©1986 by G.I.A. Publications, Inc., 7404 S. Mason Ave., Chicago, Ill. 60638.

44

Eat This Bread*

*If verses are used, the response is not repeated as an ostinato.

Words: Jacques Berthier
Music: Jacques Berthier

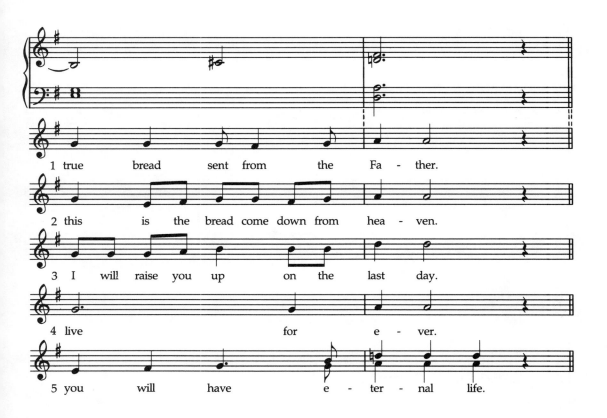

1 true bread sent from the Fa - ther.

2 this is the bread come down from hea - ven.

3 I will raise you up on the last day.

4 live for e - ver.

5 you will have e - ter - nal life.

45

On Eagle's Wings

REFRAIN

1 Rock in whom I trust!" And He will raise you up on 1 eagle's wings, bear you on the breath of dawn, make you to shine like the 1 sun, and hold you in the palm of His hand.

VERSE 2

2 The snare of the fowl-er will nev-er cap-ture you, and

63

2 fam-ine will bring you no fear: un-der His wings your

2 ref - uge, His faith-ful - ness your shield.

REFRAIN

And He will raise you up on ea - gle's wings, bear you on the

breath of dawn, make you to shine like the sun, and

VERSE 3

3 You need not fear the ter-ror of the night, nor the ar-row that flies by

3 day; though thou - sands fall a - bout you,

REFRAIN

3 near you it shall not come. And He will raise you up on

65

ea - gle's wings, bear you on the breath of dawn,

make you to shine like the sun, and hold you in the

VERSE 4

palm of His hand. 4 For to His an-gels He's

4 giv-en a com-mand to guard you in all of your ways; up-

66

REFRAIN

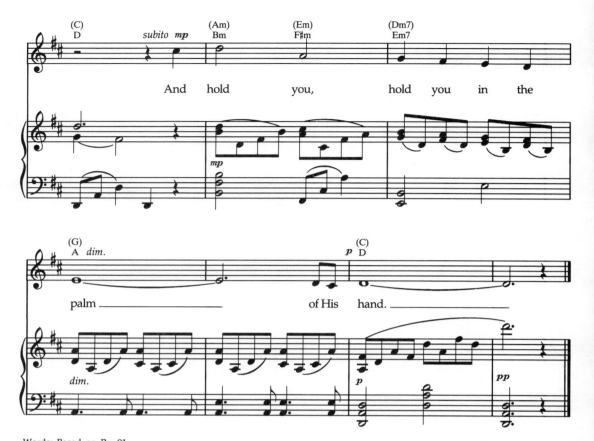

Words: Based on Ps. 91
Music: Michael Joncas
Copyright ©1979 by North American Liturgy Resources, 10802 North 23rd Avenue, Phoenix, Arizona 85029

Come to Me

46

ANTIPHON

♩. = 40

Come to me, all you who thirst: Come, and life shall be yours.

Seek and you will find, knock and the door shall be o - pened.

VERSES *(for equal voices)*

1 Take my yoke up -
2 Seek in faith the
3 Trust in me and

(to Ant.)

on you and you will find rest for your souls.
King - dom, and all will be giv - en to you.
fear not: Come, drink from the foun-tain of life.

Words: Mt 6:33, 7:7, 11:29; Jn 4:14, 7:37-38
Music: Becket Senchur, O.S.B.
Copyright ©1985, St. Vincent Archabbey, Latrobe, Pa.

47 Psalm 23: The Lord Is My Shepherd

ANTIPHON I

♩ = o of psalm

My shep - herd is the Lord, no - thing in - deed shall I want.

ANTIPHON II

♩ = o of psalm

The Lord is my shep - herd, no-thing shall I want: he

leads me by safe paths, no - thing shall I fear.

VERSES

1			My shepherd is the Lord;		there is
2	He	guides me a - long the right	path;		he is
3	You have pre -	pared a	banquet for	me	in the
4	Surely	goodness and	kindness shall	follow me	all the
5	To the	Father and	Son give	glory,		give

1 nothing I shall want.
2 true to his name.
3 sight of my foes.
4 days of my life.
5 glory to the Spirit.

If I should
My
In the
To God who

Fresh and
walk in the
head you have a-
Lord's own
is, who

green are the
valley of
nointed with
house shall I
was, and who

pastures
darkness
oil;
dwell
will be

1 where he gives me re - pose.
2 no evil would I fear.
[3
[4
[5

Near
You are

restful
there with your

1 waters he leads me, to re - vive my droop-ing spi - rit.
2 crook and your staff; with these you give me com - fort.
3 _____] my cup is o - ver - flow - ing.
4 _____] for - ev - er and ev - er.
5 _____] for - ev - er and ev - er.

48   Psalm 23: The Lord Is My Shepherd

ANTIPHON

PSALM TONE

1 The Lord *is* my shepherd;
   there is nothing *I* shall want.
   Fresh and green *are* the pastures
   where he gives *me* repose.

2 Near restful wat*ers* he leads me,
   to revive my *droop*ing spirit.
   He guides me along *the* right path;
   he is true *to* his name.

3 If I should walk in the val*ley* of darkness
   no evil *would* I fear.
   You are there with your crook *and* your staff;
   with these you *give* me comfort.

4 You have prepared a ban*quet* for me
   in the sight *of* my foes.
   My head you have anoint*ed* with oil;
   my cup is *over*flowing.

5 Surely goodness and kind*ness* shall follow me
   all the days *of* my life.
   In the Lord's own house *shall* I dwell
   for ev*er* and ever.

VERSE 2

Psalm 27: The Lord Is My Light

REFRAIN

The Lord is my light and my sal - va - tion, of whom should I be a -
fraid, of whom should I be a - fraid?

Last time rit. and Fine
(to verses)

VERSES 1, 2

1 The Lord is my light and my help; whom should I fear? The

2 There is one thing I ask of the Lord; for this I long; to

Psalm 27: The Lord Is My Light

ANTIPHON

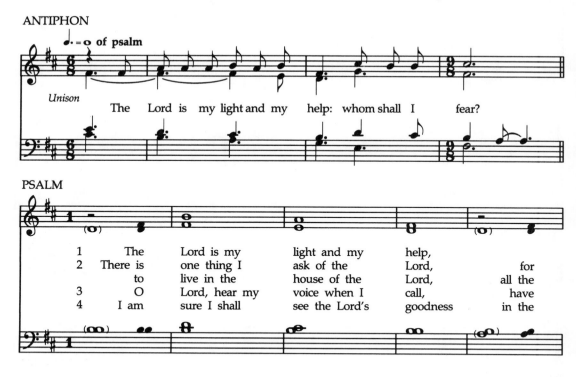

The Lord is my light and my help: whom shall I fear?

PSALM

1 The Lord is my light and my help,
2 There is one thing I ask of the Lord, for
  to live in the house of the Lord, all the
3 O Lord, hear my voice when I call, have
4 I am sure I shall see the Lord's goodness in the

1 whom shall I fear? The Lord is the stronghold of my life,
2 this I long* to savour the sweetness of the Lord,
  days of my life, to
3 mercy and answer. Of you my heart has spoken,
4 land of the living. Hope in him, hold firm and take heart.

1 before whom shall I shrink?
2 to be - hold his [ ] tem - ple.
3 "Seek his face."
4 Hope in the Lord!

*In verse 2, repeat from the beginning ("to live. . .").

Psalm 42: Like the Deer That Yearns 52

REFRAIN 1

My soul is thirst-ing for the Lord: when shall I see him face to face?

PSALM

1   Like the deer that yearns for
2 My soul is thirsting for God, the
3 My tears have be - come my bread, by
4 By day the Lord will send his

running streams, so my
God of my life; when can I
night, by day, as I hear it
loving kindness; by night I will

soul is yearning for you, my God.
enter and see the face of God?
said all day long; "Where is your God?"
sing to him, praise the God of my life.

Psalms 42 and 43: Like the Deer That Longs

INTRODUCTION

Soprano Descant

longs for run - ning streams, my soul. _____

REFRAIN

Like the deer that longs for run-ning streams, my soul longs for you my God.

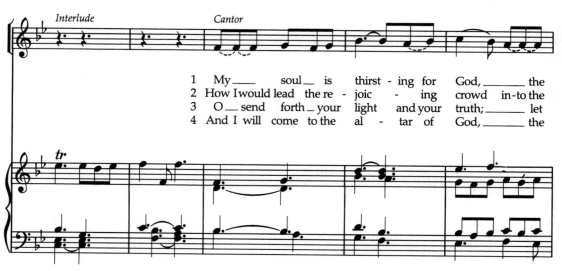

Interlude   *Cantor*

1 My ____ soul __ is thirst - ing for God, _____ the
2 How I would lead the re - joic - ing crowd in-to the
3 O __ send forth __ your light and your truth; _____ let
4 And I will come to the al - tar of God, _____ the

God of my life; when___ can I en - ter___
house___ of God, a - mid cries___ of glad - ness and
these be my guide. Let them bring___ me to your
God of my joy. My re - deem - er, I will

and___ see the face___ of God?
thanks - giv - ing, the throng_ wild_ with joy.
ho - ly moun - tain___ to the place where you dwell.
thank you on the harp, ___ O___ God,_ my God.

to refrain

CODA *after stanza 4 and refrain:*

Psalm 63: In the Shadow of Your Wings

ANTIPHON

In the sha-dow of your wings I sing for joy.

VERSES

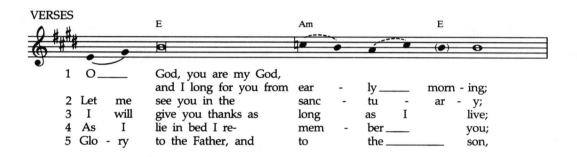

1 O___ God, you are my God,
    and I long for you from ear - ly___ morn - ing;
2 Let me see you in the sanc - tu - ar - y;
3 I will give you thanks as long as I live;
4 As I lie in bed I re- mem - ber___ you;
5 Glo - ry to the Father, and to the___ son,

1 My whole being de - sires___ you;
2 let me see how mighty and glo - ri - ous you are.
3 I will raise my hands to you___ in prayer.
4 all night long I think of you,
    because you have al - ways been my help.
5 and to the Ho - ly Spir - it.

1 like a dry, worn-out and wa - ter - less land,
2 Your constant love is better than life it - self,
3 My soul will feast and be sat - is - fied,
4 In the shadow of your wings I sing for joy.
5 As it was in the be- gin - ning, is now,

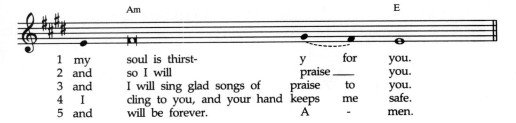

1 my	soul is thirst-		y	for	you.
2 and	so I will		praise ___		you.
3 and	I will sing glad songs of		praise	to	you.
4 I	cling to you, and your hand	keeps		me	safe.
5 and	will be forever.		A	-	men.

Words: From the *Good News Bible*, copyright ©1976, the American Bible Society
Music: Michael Joncas, copyright ©1979, G.I.A. Publications, Inc. All rights reserved.

Psalm 63: My Soul Is Thirsting

My soul is thirst-ing for you, O

Lord, thirst-ing for you my God.

Ps. 62(63), 2. 3-4. 5-6. 8-9

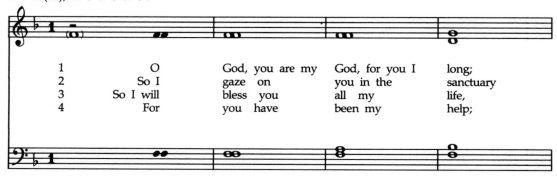

1	O	God, you are my	God, for you I	long;
2	So I	gaze on	you in the	sanctuary
3	So I will	bless you	all my	life,
4	For	you have	been my	help;

for	you my	soul is	thirsting.
to	see your	strength and your	glory.
in your	name I will	lift up my	hands.
in the	shadow of your	wings I re-	joice.

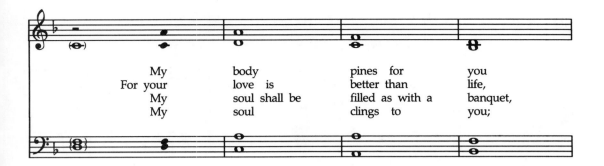

My	body	pines for	you
For your	love is	better than	life,
My	soul shall be	filled as with a	banquet,
My	soul	clings to	you;

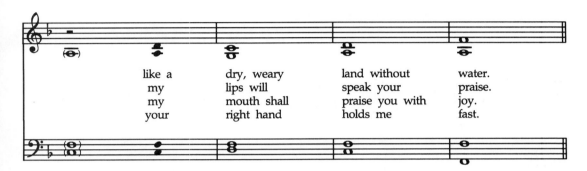

like a	dry, weary	land without	water.
my	lips will	speak your	praise.
my	mouth shall	praise you with	joy.
your	right hand	holds me	fast.

56

Psalm 84
How Lovely Is Your Dwelling Place

REFRAIN

How love-ly is your dwell-ing place. O Lord of Hosts! Lord of Hosts!

VERSES

1 How love-ly is your dwelling place, O Lord of Hosts!
2 The spar-row even finds a home,
3 How hap-py they who dwell in your house, O Lord!
4 O Lord of Hosts, listen to my prayer,

My soul grows weak with longing for the courts of the Lord;
The swal-low finds a nest wherein to place her young;
Un-ceas-ing-ly they sing your praise;
Bend down your ear, O God of Ja - cob;

My heart and flesh they thrill for joy.
Near to your altars, Lord of Hosts.
How happy they that draw their strength from you.
Be - hold, O God our shield,

Joy   in the   liv   -   ing   God.
My   King,   my   God!
When   they have set their heart on sacred   pil   -   grim   - age.
Look   on the face of your a-   noint -   ed   one.

Words: Stephen Somerville
Music: Stephen Somerville, copyright ©Rev. Stephen Somerville. All rights reserved.

Psalm 103: The Lord Is Kind

ANTIPHON

The Lord is kind and mer - ci - ful.
mer - ci - ful.

VERSES

1 My __ soul, __ give thanks to the Lord, all my
2 It is **God** who for - gives all your guilt, who __
3 The __ Lord is com - pas - sion and love, slow to
4 As __ far as the east is from west so __

be - ing, bless God's ho - ly name. My __ soul, _____ give thanks to the
heals __ all your ills, _____ who re - deems _____ your life from the
an - ger, rich in mer - cy, treats us not _____ ac - cor - ding to
far does God re - move our sins. As a fa - ther has re - gard for his

Lord and __ ne - ver for - get __ all his bless - ings.
grave, who __ crowns you with love __ and com - pas - sion.
sin nor re - pays us ac - cor - ding to our faults. __
sons, the __ Lord will for - give __ those who re- vere him.

Psalm 103: The Lord Is Kind

ANTIPHON

The Lord is kind and mer-ci-ful. The Lord is kind and mer-ci-ful.

VERSE 1

1 My soul, give thanks to the Lord, all my

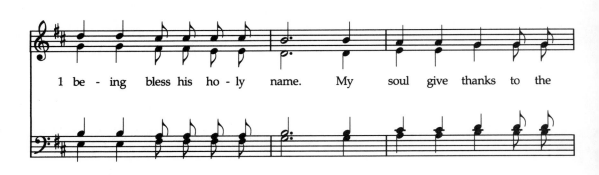

1 be - ing bless his ho - ly name. My soul give thanks to the

To Antiphon

1 Lord, and nev - er for - get all his bless - ings.

VERSE 2

2 It is he who for - gives all your guilt, who

2 heals ev - 'ry one of your ills, who re - deems your life from the

To Antiphon

2 grave, who crowns you with love and com - pas - sion.

VERSE 3

3 The Lord is com - pas - sion and love, slow to

3 an - ger and rich in mer - cy. His

3 wrath will come to an end; he will not be an - gry for

3 ev - er. He does not treat us ac - cord - ing to our

To Antiphon

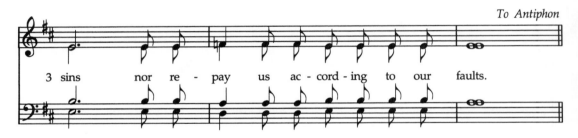

3 sins nor re - pay us ac - cord - ing to our faults.

59 Psalm 103: The Lord Is Tender and Caring

ANTIPHON
Optional Descant

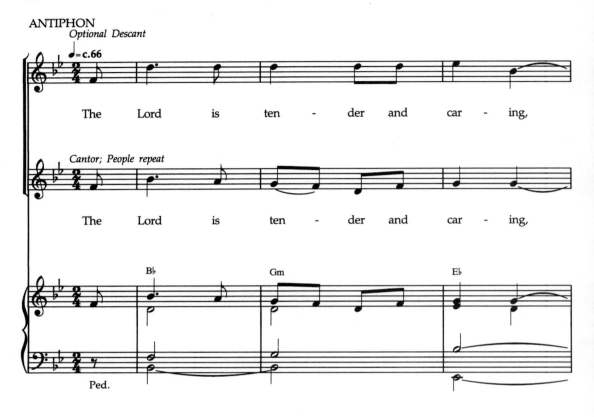

The Lord is ten - der and car - ing,

Cantor; People repeat

The Lord is ten - der and car - ing,

slow to an - ger, rich in love.

slow to an - ger, rich in love.

PSALM TONE

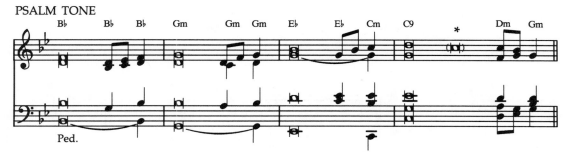

*If reaching the D is difficult, the singer(s) and organist may choose the C.

1 The Lord is tender and caring,→
slow to anger, *rich* in love.
God will not accuse us long,→
nor hold our *sins* for trial,
nor exact from *us* in kind
what our *sins* deserve.

2 As tender as fath*er* to child,
so gentle is God *to* believers.
God knows how *we* are made,
remembers *we* are dust.

3 Our days pass *by* like grass,
our prime like a flow*er* in bloom.
A wind comes, the *flow*er goes,
empty *now* its place.

4 God's love is *from* all time,
God's justice be*yond* all time,
for believers of each *gen*eration:
those who keep the covenant,→
who take care to *live* the law.

Words: Copyright ©1969, 1980, ICEL
Music: Howard Hughes, s.m., copyright ©1983, ICEL

60 See What Goodness*

*This text appears in hymn form, with alternate tunes, at number 87.

Cantor

1 Blest be God, by whose great mer - cy We are bap - tized
2 We are made in God's own im - age; On us is the
3 Res - cued from the pow'r of dark - ness, Brought in - to re -

in the Son. Set a - part as ho - ly peo - ple,
Spir - it poured. We are cleansed in sav - ing wa - ter;
splen - dent light, Of - fer thanks for lov - ing mer - cy;

We are God's and not our own.
We are clothed in Christ the Lord.
Praise for gen - tle - ness and might!

Notes:

The refrain is intended to be sung by everyone and the stanzas by Cantor or Choir.

The organ interlude is intended to be played after each of the stanzas.

The entire hymn may be accompanied by organ only. The introduction is scored for two flutes, cello, string bass and organ, or may be played by organ alone.

Text: Delores Dufner, o.s.b., copyright ©1984, the Sisters of St. Benedict, St. Joseph, Minn. 56374
Tune: DANCER 87.87.D, copyright ©1984, Jay Hunstiger, 4545 Wichita Trail, Medina, Minn. 55340

The Cry of the Poor

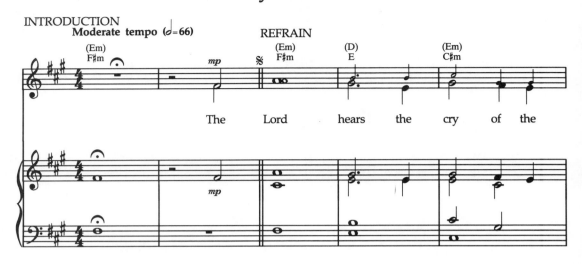

INTRODUCTION
Moderate tempo (♩=66)   REFRAIN

The Lord hears the cry of the

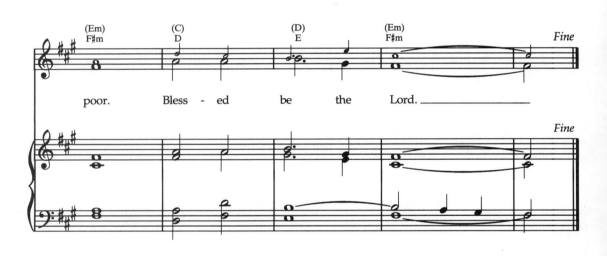

poor. Bless - ed be the Lord. _____

Fine

VERSES Slightly faster (♩=76)

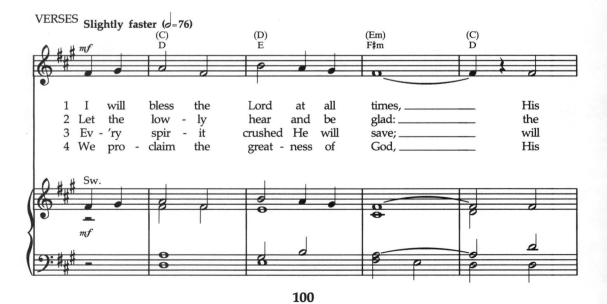

1 I will bless the Lord at all times, _____ His
2 Let the low - ly hear and be glad: _____ the
3 Ev - 'ry spir - it crushed He will save; _____ will
4 We pro - claim the great - ness of God, _____ His

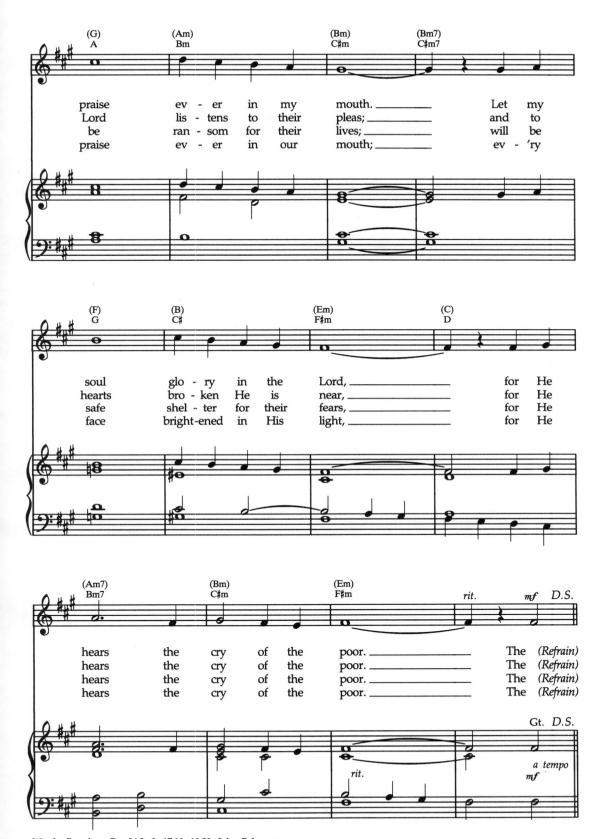

praise ev - er in my mouth._____ Let my
Lord lis - tens to their pleas;_____ and to
be ran - som for their lives;_____ will be
praise ev - er in our mouth;_____ ev - 'ry

soul glo - ry in the Lord,_____ for He
hearts bro - ken He is near,_____ for He
safe shel - ter for their fears,_____ for He
face bright-ened in His light,_____ for He

hears the cry of the poor._____ The (Refrain)
hears the cry of the poor._____ The (Refrain)
hears the cry of the poor._____ The (Refrain)
hears the cry of the poor._____ The (Refrain)

Words: Based on Pss 34:2, 3; 17:18; 19:23. John Foley, s.j.
Music: John Foley, s.j.

This Alone

For one day with-in Your tem - ple heals
ev - 'ry day a - lone. O Lord, bring me to Your
dwell - ing. 2 The

to Verses

VERSE 1

1 Hear, O Lord, the sound of my

103

1 call - ing. Hear, O Lord, and
1 show me Your way.

to Antiphon II

VERSE 2

2 Lord is my light and hope of sal -
2 va - tion. The Lord is my ref - uge;

ANTIPHON III

105

tem - ple heals ev - 'ry day a - lone. O

Lord, bring me to Your dwell -

ing.

8',4',2'

Sw.

no Ped.

VERSE 3

3 Wait on the Lord, and hope in His

106

3 mer - cy. Wait on the Lord, and

3 live in His love.

to Antiphon IV

rit.

ANTIPHON IV

One thing I ask, this a - lone I

Gt.

Ped.

seek, to dwell in the house of the Lord all my

Words: Based on Ps. 27. Tim Manion
Music: Tim Manion, copyright ©1981, Tim Manion and North American Liturgy Resources,
   10802 North 23rd Avenue, Phoenix, Arizona 85029. All rights reserved. Used with permission.

You Are Near

VERSES 1 and 3

1 Lord, You have searched my ___ heart, and You
3 You know my heart and its ways, You who

Man.

1 know when I sit and when I stand. Your ___ hand is up-on me pro-
3 formed me be-fore ___ I was born in the se-cret of dark-ness be-

1 tect-ing me from death, keep-ing me from harm. _____ (Antiphon)
3 fore I saw the sun in my moth-er's womb. _____ (Antiphon)

110

VERSES 2 and 4

2 Where can I run from Your love? If I
4 Mar-vel-ous to me are Your works; how pro-

2 climb to the hea-vens, You are there; If I
4 found are Your thoughts, __ my __ Lord. E - ven

2 'fly to the sun-rise or sail be-yond the sea,
4 if I could count them, they num-ber as the stars,

2 still I'd find You there. (Antiphon)
4 You would still be there. (Antiphon)

Words: Based on Psalm 139. Daniel Schutte, s.j.
Music: Daniel Schutte, s.j.

All Creatures of Our God and King

(Higher keys at numbers 65 and 66)

1 All crea-tures of our God and King, lift up your voic-es, let us
2 All you with mer-cy in your heart, for-giv-ing o-thers, take your
3 And e-ven you, most gen-tle death, wait-ing to hush our fi-nal
4 Let all things their cre-a-tor bless, and wor-ship him in hum-ble-

sing: Al-le-lu-ia, al-le-lu-ia! Bright burn-ing
part, O__ sing now: Al-le-lu-ia! All you that
breath, O__ praise him, Al-le-lu-ia! You lead back
ness, O__ praise him, Al-le-lu-ia! Praise God the

sun with gold-en beams, pale sil-ver moon that gen-tly gleams,
pain and sor-row bear, praise God, and cast on him your care:
home the child of God, for Christ our Lord that way has trod:
Fa-ther, praise the Son, and praise the Spi-rit, Three in One:

O praise him, O praise him, Al - le - lu - ia,
al - le - lu - ia, al - le - lu - ia!

Text: Francis of Assisi 1182–1226; tr. William H. Draper, 1855–1933, alt.
Tune: LASST UNS ERFREUEN 888.888 with alleluia, *Geistliche Kirchengesänge*, Köln, 1623
Setting from *The English Hymnal* by Ralph Vaughan Williams, copyright ©Oxford University Press. Used by permission.
   Not for sale outside the U.S.A.

65 All You on Earth

(Lower key at number 64)

1 All you on earth, re-joice and sing; Give glo-ry to our ris-en
2 Your death, O Lord, was but the seed From which a new life would pro-
3 The Lord has made this spe-cial day; To joy let sor-row now give

King! Raise your voic - es! Al - le - lu - ia! Our Lord, who
ceed! Al - le - lu - ia, al - le - lu - ia! Our Lord, who
way! Cel - e - brate it! Al - le - lu - ia! All Chris-tians,

died, now tru - ly lives; To us this prom-ise he now gives.
rose by his own pow'r, Will raise us all in that last hour.
who one faith de - clare, Sing praise to him whose life we share.

REFRAIN

Al - le - lu - ia, al - le - lu - ia, al - le - lu - ia,

al - le - lu - ia, al - le - lu - ia!

Text: Omer Westendorf, b. 1916, copyright ©1970, World Library Publications, Inc.
Tune: LASST UNS ERFREUEN 888.888 with alleluia, *Geistliche Kirchengesänge*, Köln, 1623
Setting from *The English Hymnal*, copyright ©Oxford University Press. Used by permission.

66 Now All the Vault of Heaven Resounds

(Lower key at number 64)

1 Now all the vault of heav'n re - sounds In praise of love that
2 E - ter-nal is the gift he brings, There - fore our heart with
3 Oh, fill us, Lord, with daunt-less love; Set heart and will on
4 A - dor-ing prais - es now we bring And with the heav'n-ly

still a - bounds: "Christ has tri - umphed! He is liv - ing!"
rap-ture sings: "Christ has tri - umphed! He is liv - ing!"
things a - bove That we con - quer through your tri - umph;
bless-ed sing: "Christ has tri - umphed! Al - le - lu - ia!"

Sing, choirs of an - gels, loud and clear! Re - peat their song
Now still he comes to give us life And by his pres -
Grant grace suf - fi - cient for life's day That by our lives
Be to the Fa - ther and our Lord, To Spir - it blest,

of glo - ry here: "Christ has tri - umphed! Christ has tri - umphed!"
ence stills all strife. Christ has tri - umphed! He is liv - ing!
we tru - ly say: "Christ has tri - umphed! He is liv - ing!"
most ho - ly God, All the glo - ry, nev - er end - ing!

Al - le - lu – ia, al - le - lu – ia, al - le - lu – ia!

Text: Paul Z. Strodach, 1876–1947, alt., copyright ©1958, *Service Book and Hymnal*
   Used by permission of Augsburg Publishing House.
Tune: LASST UNS ERFREUEN 888.888 with alleluia, *Geistliche Kirchengesänge*, Köln, 1623
   Setting from *The English Hymnal*, copyright ©Oxford University Press. Used by permission. Not for sale outside the U.S.A.

67 Love Divine, All Loves Excelling

(Lower key at number 68)

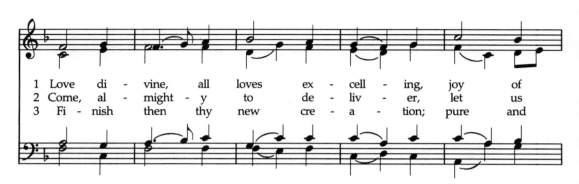

1 Love di - vine, all loves ex - cell - ing, joy of
2 Come, al - might - y to de - liv - er, let us
3 Fi - nish then thy new cre - a - tion; pure and

heaven, to earth come down, fix in us thy
all thy life re - ceive; sud - den - ly re -
spot - less let us be; let us see thy

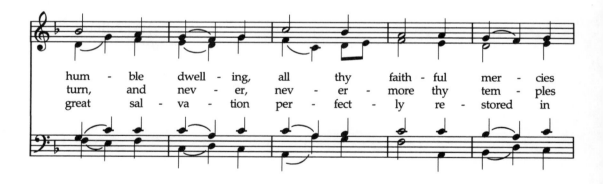

hum - ble dwell - ing, all thy faith - ful mer - cies
turn, and nev - er, nev - er - more thy tem - ples
great sal - va - tion per - fect - ly re - stored in

crown. Je - sus, thou art all com - pas - sion, pure, un -
leave. Thee we would be al - way bless - ing, serve thee
thee: changed from glo - ry in - to glo - ry, till in

bound - ed love thou art; vis - it us with
as thy hosts a - bove, pray, and praise with thee
heaven we take our place, till we cast our

thy sal - va - tion, en - ter ev - ery trem - bling heart.
with - out ceas - ing, glo - ry in thy pre - cious love.
crowns be - fore thee, lost in won - der, love, and praise.

Text: Charles Wesley, 1701–1788
Tune: HYFRYDOL 87.87.D, Rowland H. Prichard, 1811–1887

68

Alleluia! Sing to Jesus

(Higher key at number 67)

1 Al - le - lu - ia! sing to Je - sus!
2 Al - le - lu - ia! not as or - phans
3 Al - le - lu - ia! bread of an - gels,
4 Al - le - lu - ia King e - ter - nal

His the scep - ter, his the throne;
are we left in sor - row now;
and on earth our food, our stay;
you the Lord of lords we own;

Al - le - lu - ia! his the tri - umph,
Al - le - lu - ia! he is near us,
Al - le - lu - ia! here the sin - ful
Al - le - lu - ia! born of Mar - y

His the vic - to - ry a - lone:
faith be - lieves, nor ques - tions how;
flee to you from day to day:
earth, your foot - stool, heav'n your throne:

Hark! the songs of peace - ful Zi - on
Though the cloud from sight re - ceived him,
In - ter - ces - sor, friend of sin - ners,
You with in the veil have en - tered,

thun - der like a might - y flood;
when the for - ty days were o'er,
earth's Re - deem - er plead for me,
robed in flesh, our great high priest;

Je - sus out of ev - ry na - tion
Shall our hearts for - get his pro - mise,
Where the songs of all the sin - less
You on earth both priest and vic - tim

has re - deemed us by his blood.
"I am with you ev - er - more"?
sweep a - cross the crys - tal sea.
in the eu - cha - ris - tic feast.

Text: William Chatterton Dix, 1837–1898
HYFRYDOL 87.87.D, Rowland Hugh Prichard, 1811–1887

121

Jesus Christ Is Risen Today

1 Jesus Christ is ris'n to-day,
2 Hymns of praise then let us sing,
3 But the pains which he en-dured,
4 Sing we to our God a-bove.

Alleluia!

Our tri-umph-ant ho - ly day,
Un - to Christ, our heav'n - ly King,
Our sal - va - tion have pro-cured;
Praise e - ter - nal as his love;

Alleluia!

Who did once up - on the cross,
Who en - dured the cross and grave,
Now a - bove the sky he's King,
Praise him, all you heav'n-ly host.

Alleluia!

Suf - fer to re - deem our loss.
Sin - ners to re - deem and save.
Where the an - gels ev - er sing.
Fa - ther Son and Ho - ly Ghost.

Alleluia!

Text: v. 1, *Lyra Davidica*, 1708, alt.; vss. 2, 3, John Arnold, 1749, alt.; v. 4, Charles Wesley, 1749
Tune: EASTER HYMN 77.77 with alleluias. *Lyra Davidica*, 1708.

Come to Me*

Cantor or choir

1 Come to Me, all who are thirst-y, Drink the wa-ter I will give.
2 Come to Me, all who would wor-ship, Would in truth and spir-it pray.
3 Come to Me, all who are wea-ry, Come that I may give you rest.
4 Come to Me, all who are seek-ing; Let your hearts hear what I say:

If you knew what gift I of-fer, You would come to Me and live.
If you seek to know the Fa-ther, Come to Me; I am the Way.
Eat the bread that I will give you; At this ban-quet be my guest.
Those who drink the blood I share now, Shall have life on that last day.

All

Bless-ed Je-sus, lov-ing Sav-ior, Give us wa-ter from this well.
Bless-ed Je-sus, lov-ing Sav-ior, Show your kind-ness to our race.
Bless-ed Je-sus, lov-ing Sav-ior, Let us taste the liv-ing bread.
Lov-ing Sav-ior, you have taught us All that we be-lieve and know.

*This text may be sung to HOLY MANNA (no. 70A),
    PLEADING SAVIOR (no. 70B), or other tunes of 87.87.D meter.

Lord of mer - cy, by your good-ness We have joy no tongue can tell.
Lord of mer - cy, in your good-ness Let us see the Fa - ther's face.
Lord of mer - cy, in your good-ness By your bo - dy we are fed.
Bless-ed Je - sus, if we leave you, Lord, to whom, then, shall we go?

1 *(Interlude A)*
3 *(Interlude A)*

2 *(Interlude B)*

4 *(Interlude C)*

Cantor or choir

5 Come to Me and I will heal you, Give for sin God's sav - ing grace.

I have lived on earth be-fore you; Now a-bove I save your place.

Descant

Bless-ed Je - sus, lov - ing Sav - ior, Broth - er of friends!

Melody (All)

Bless-ed Je - sus, lov - ing Sav - ior, Best of broth-ers and of friends!

Lord of mer-cy, in your good-ness, Give joy that ne - ver ends.

Lord of mer-cy, in your good-ness, Give us joy that ne - ver ends.

Text: Delores Dufner, o.s.b., copyright ©1982, Sisters of St. Benedict, St. Joseph, Minn. 56374
Tune: 87.87.D, copyright ©1982, Jay Hunstiger, 4545 Wichita Trail, Medina, Minn. 55340

Come to Me

70A

Alternate Tune

Tune: HOLY MANNA 87.87.D, *Columbia Harmony*, 1825, attr. to William Moore

Come to Me

Alternate Tune

(Lower key at number 99B)

Tune: PLEADING SAVIOR, 87.87.D, *Plymouth Collection*, New York, 1855

71 Come, You Thankful People, Come

1 Come, you thank-ful peo - ple, come, Raise the song of har - vest home;
2 All the world is God's own field, Fruit un - to his praise to yield;
3 For the Lord our God shall come, And shall take his har - vest home;
4 E - ven so, Lord, quick - ly come To your fi - nal har - vest home;

All is safe - ly gath - ered in, Ere the win - ter storms be - gin;
Wheat and tares to - geth - er sown, Un - to joy or sor - row grown;
From his field shall in that day All of - fens - es purge a - way;
Gath - er all your peo - ple in, Free from sor - row, free from sin;

God, our Mak - er, does pro - vide For our wants to be sup - plied;
First the blade, and then the ear, Then the full corn shall ap - pear:
Give his an - gels charge at last In the fire the tares to cast,
There, for ev - er pu - ri - fied, In your pres-ence to a - bide:

Come to God's own tem - ple, come, Raise the song of har - vest home.
Grant, O har - vest Lord, that we Whole-some grain and pure may be.
But the fruit - ful ears to store In his gar - ner ev - er - more.
Come, with all your an - gels, come, Raise the glo-rious har - vest - home.

Text: Henry Alford, 1810–1871
Tune: ST. GEORGE'S WINDSOR 77.77.D, George Job Elvey, 1816–1893

For All the Saints

(Lower key at number 90)

72

1 For all the saints who from their la-bors rest, who
2 O blest com-mun - ion, fel-low-ship di - vine!_____
3 But lo! there breaks a yet more glo-rious day; the
4 From earth's wide bounds, from o-cean's far-thest coast, through

thee_____ by faith be - fore the world con - fessed, thy
We feeb-ly strug - gle, they in glo - ry shine; yet
saints_____ tri - umph - ant rise in bright ar - ray; the
gates_____ of pearl stream in the count-less host,_____

Name, O_____ Je - sus, be for ev - er blessed.
all are_____ one in thee for all are thine.
King of_____ glo - ry pass - es on his way.
sing - ing to Fa - ther, Son and Ho - ly Ghost,

Al - le - lu - ia, al - le - lu - ia!

Text: William Walsham How, 1823–1897
Tune: SINE NOMINE, 10.10.10 with alleluias, Ralph Vaughan Williams, 1872–1958
From *The English Hymnal*, copyright ℗Oxford University Press. Not for sale outside the U.S.A.

73

Jerusalem, My Happy Home

(Lower key at number 103A)

1 Je - ru - sa - lem, my hap - py home, When
2 O hap - py har - bor of the saints, O
3 Thy gar - dens and thy gal - lant walks Con -
4 There trees for ev - er - more bear fruit And

shall I come to thee? When shall my sor - rows
sweet and pleas - ant soil! In thee no sor - row
tin - ual - ly are green; There grow such sweet and
ev - er - more do spring; There ev - er - more the

have an end? Thy joys when shall I see?
may be found, No grief, no care, no toil.
pleas - ant flow'rs As no - where else are seen.
an - gels sit And ev - er - more do sing.

5 Jerusalem, Jerusalem, God grant that I may see
Thine endless joy, and of the same, Partaker ever be!

Text: F.B.P. in the *Song of Mary*, 1601
Tune: LAND OF REST, C.M., trad. American melody, acc. by Sister Theophane Hytrek, O.S.F., 1980, copyright ©1980, ICEL

74

Sing of Christ, Proclaim His Glory

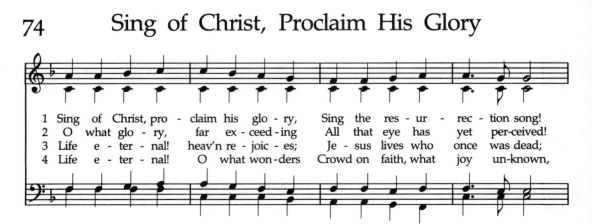

1 Sing of Christ, pro - claim his glo - ry, Sing the res - ur - rec - tion song!
2 O what glo - ry, far ex - ceed - ing All that eye has yet per-ceived!
3 Life e - ter - nal! heav'n re - joic - es; Je - sus lives who once was dead;
4 Life e - ter - nal! O what won-ders Crowd on faith, what joy un-known,

Death and sor - row, earth's dark sto - ry, To the form - er
Ho - liest hearts for a - ges plead - ing, Nev - er that full
Join with all the heav'n - ly voic - es; Child of God, lift
When, a - mid earth's clos - ing thun - ders, Saints shall stand be -

days be - long. All a - round the clouds are break - ing.
joy con - ceived. God has prom - ised, Christ pre - pares it,
up your head! Pa - triarchs from the dis - tant a - ges,
fore the throne! O to en - ter that bright por - tal,

Soon the storms of time shall cease; In God's like - ness,
There on high our wel - come waits; Ev - 'ry hum - ble
Saints all long - ing for their heav'n, Proph - ets, psalm - ists,
See that glow - ing fir - ma - ment, Know, with you O

peo - ple wak - ing, Know the ev - er - last - ing peace.
spir - it shares it, Christ has passed th'e - ter - nal gates.
seers, and sa - ges, All a - wait the glo - ry giv'n.
God im - mor - tal, Je - sus Christ whom you have sent!

Text: 1 Cor. 15:20, William Josiah Irons, 1812–1883
Tune: HYMN TO JOY, 87.87.D, adapted in 1846 by Edward Hodges, 1796–1867, from Ludwig van Beethoven, 1770–1827

131

75   All Who Seek To Know*

1 All who seek to know and serve God, See the past and un-der-stand:
2 If our God does not con-demn us, Who a-gainst us then will stand?
3 Al-le-lu-ia, al-le-lu-ia! Joy a-waits all those who mourn.

None who hoped were dis-ap-point-ed; Rich the bless-ings from His hand!
Will the Lord, who died for sin-ners, Who sits now at God's right hand?
Al-le-lu-ia, al-le-lu-ia! Death has died and life is born.

None who wait-ed were for-sa-ken; None who trust-ed were de-ceived.
What could take us from Christ Je-sus? Nei-ther hun-ger, sword, nor pain!
Al-le-lu-ia, al-le-lu-ia! Our re-deem-er, Je-sus lives!

All who asked His gra-cious par-don, Gen-tle mer-cy have re-ceived.
Nei-ther life nor death shall part us From the Lamb for us once slain.
Al-le-lu-ia, al-le-lu-ia! Grace and glo-ry Je-sus gives!

*This text may also be sung to ODE TO JOY (no. 74), HYFRYDOL (no. 67),
PLEADING SAVIOR (no. 70B), or other tunes of 87.87.D meter.

Text: Delores Dufner, o.s.b., copyright ©1983, the Sisters of St. Benedict, St. Joseph, Minn. 56374
Tune: 87.87.D, copyright ©1983, Jay Hunstiger, 4545 Wichita Trail, Medina, Minn. 55340

76 My Shepherd Will Supply My Need

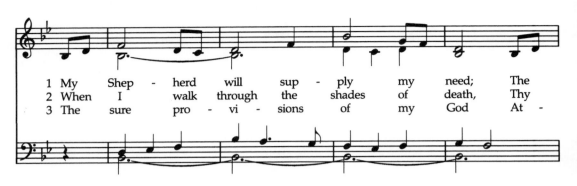

1 My Shep - herd will sup - ply my need; The
2 When I walk through the shades of death, Thy
3 The sure pro - vi - sions of my God At -

Lord God is his name. _____ In pas - tures green he
pres - ence is my stay; _____ One word of thy sup -
tend me all my days; _____ O may thy house be

makes me feed, Be - side the liv - ing stream. _____ He
port - ing breath Drives all my fears a - way. _____ Thy
my a - bode, And all my work be praise! _____ There

brings my wan - d'ring spir - it back, When I for -
hand, in sight of all my foes, Does still my
would I find a set - tled rest, While oth - ers

sake his ways; _____ And leads me for his
ta - ble spread; _____ My cup with bless - ings
go and come, _____ No more a stran - ger

mer - cy's sake, In paths of truth and grace. _____
o - ver - flows, Thine oil a - noints my head. _____
nor a guest; But like a child at home. _____

Text: Psalm 22(23), Isaac Watts, 1674–1748, alt.
Tune: RESIGNATION, C.M.D., *Southern Harmony*, 1835, acc. by Sister Theophane Hytrek, o.s.f., 1980, copyright ©1980 ICEL

Merciful Savior

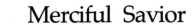

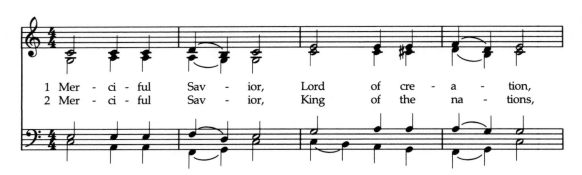

1 Mer - ci - ful Sav - ior, Lord of cre - a - tion,
2 Mer - ci - ful Sav - ior, King of the na - tions,

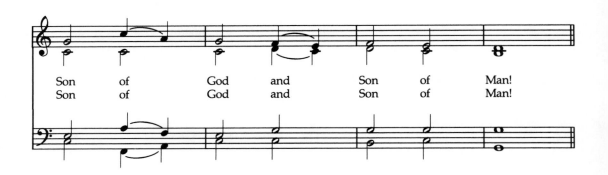

Son of God and Son of Man!
Son of God and Son of Man!

Je - sus, we love you, Serve and o - bey you,
Glo - ry and hon - or, Praise, ad - o - ra - tion,

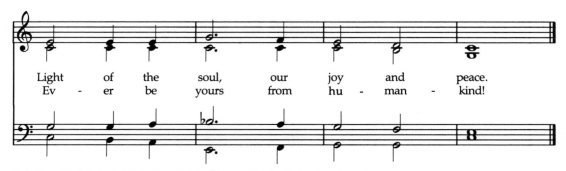

Light of the soul, our joy and peace.
Ev - er be yours from hu - man - kind!

Text: Irwin Udulutsch, O.F.M. CAP., copyright ©1959, 1977, The Order of St. Benedict, Inc.
Tune: ST. ELIZABETH, Irreg., *Schlesische Volkslieder*, 1842

78   Now Thank We All Our God

love, And still is ours to - day.
sin, Till heav - en we pos - sess.
now, And shall be ev - er - more.

Text: Martin Rinkart, 1586–1649, tr. by Catherine Winkworth, 1827–1878
Tune: NUN DANKET 67.67.66.66, Johann Cruger, 1598—1662

O Christ, Our Hope 79

1 O Christ, our hope, our hearts' de - sire, Re - demp - tion's on - ly
2 How vast the mer - cy and the love Which led you to the
3 But now the bonds of death are burst, The ran - som has been
4 O may your might - y love pre - vail Our sin - ful souls to

spring; Cre - a - tor of the world are you Its
tree, And on this cross you died for us To
paid; and you are on your Fa - ther's throne In
spare, O may we come be - fore your throne And

Sav - ior and its King, Its Sav - ior and its King.
set your peo - ple free, To set your peo - ple free.
maj - es - ty ar - rayed, In maj - es - ty ar - rayed.
find ac - cept - ance there, And find ac - cept-ance there!

Text: Jesu, nostra redemptio, 8th c., tr. John Chandler, 1806–1876
Tune: LOBT GOTT IHR CHRISTEN (Hermann), 8.6.88.6, Nikolaus Hermann, c. 1485–1561. Arr. J.S. Bach, 1685–1750

Of You My Heart Is Speaking*

1 Of You my heart is speak - ing: "O seek to know the Lord!"
2 The swal - low finds with You, Lord, Safe - keep - ing for its nest.
3 If I seek first the king - dom, All else will then be mine.

For You my soul is thirst - ing: Drink deep - ly of God's Word!
With - in Your ho - ly dwell - ing Is my e - ter - nal rest.
And if I fol - low Je - sus, In glo - ry I will shine.

Where - ev - er is my trea - sure, My heart will al - so be.
O heart, be not so fear - ful: God's man - sion you will share.
My broth - er and my sav - ior Pre - pares for me a place.

O let it be with You, Lord, For all e - ter - ni - ty!
Your Lord has gone be - fore you, And now a - waits you there.
On wak - ing I shall greet You, In joy be - hold Your face.

(Final stanza F♯ in tenor)

*This text may be sung to AURELIA (no. 80A), ELLACOMBE (no. 80B),
    or other tunes of 76.76.D meter.

Text: Delores Dufner, O.S.B., copyright ©1983, the Sisters of St. Benedict, St. Joseph, Minn. 56374
Tune: 76.76.D, copyright ©1983, Jay Hunstiger, 4545 Wichita Trail, Medina, Minn. 55340

Of You My Heart Is Speaking

Alternate Tune

(Higher key at number 94A)

Tune: AURELIA 76.76.D, Samuel Sebastian Wesley, 1864

Of You My Heart Is Speaking   8OB

Alternate Tune

(Higher key at number 91)

Tune: ELLACOMBE C.M.D. Melody from *Gesangbuch. . . der Herzogl. Wirtembergischen Katholischen Hofkapelle*, Würtemberg, 1784, arr. in *Hymns Ancient and Modern*, 1861

81   O Glorify the Lord*

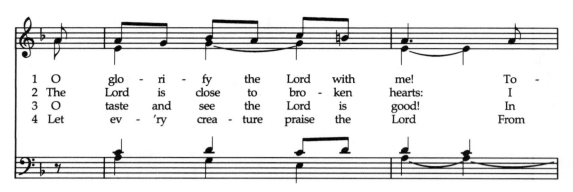

1 O glo - ri - fy the Lord with me! To -
2 The Lord is close to bro - ken hearts: I
3 O taste and see the Lord is good! In
4 Let ev - 'ry crea - ture praise the Lord From

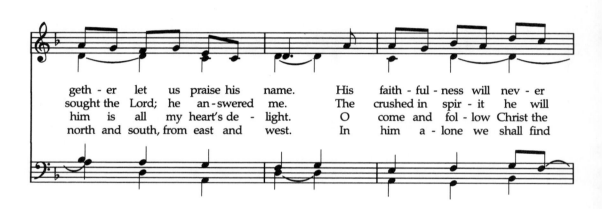

geth - er let us praise his name. His faith - ful - ness will nev - er
sought the Lord; he an - swered me. The crushed in spir - it he will
him is all my heart's de - light. O come and fol - low Christ the
north and south, from east and west. In him a - lone we shall find

end; In ev - 'ry age he is the same.
save: From all my fears he set me free.
Lord, That you may share his glo - ry bright.
joy; In him a - lone, e - ter - nal rest.

5 At all times let us bless the Lord,
And ever on our lips his praise.
Let us give thanks for mercies past,
And glorify him all our days!

*This text may be sung to OLD HUNDREDTH (no. 81A) or JESU, DULCIS MEMORIA (no. 81B)
or other tunes of Long Meter.

Text: Adapted from Ps. 34, Delores Dufner, o.s.b., copyright ©1982, the Sisters of St. Benedict, St. Joseph, Minn. 56374
Tune: 8.8.8.8., copyright ©1982, Jay Hunstiger, 4545 Wichita Trail, Medina, Minn. 55340

O Glorify the Lord

Alternate Tune

Tune: OLD 100TH, L.M., Louis Bourgeois, c. 1510–1561, in *Genevan Psalter*, 1551

O Glorify the Lord

Alternate Tune

Tune: JESU, DULCIS MEMORIA, L.M., Plainchant, mode I, acc. by Theodore Marier, 1980

O God, Our Help in Ages Past

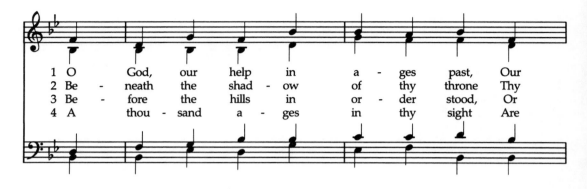

1 O God, our help in a - ges past, Our
2 Be - neath the shad - ow of thy throne Thy
3 Be - fore the hills in or - der stood, Or
4 A thou - sand a - ges in thy sight Are

hope for years to come, Our shel - ter from the
saints have dwelt se - cure; Suf - fi - cient is thine
earth re - ceived her frame, From ev - er - last - ing
like an eve - ning gone: Short as the watch that

storm - y blast, And our e - ter - nal home!
arm a - lone, And our de - fence is sure.
thou art God, To end - less years the same.
ends the night Be - fore the ri - sing sun.

5 O God, our help in ages past,
Our hope for years to come;
Be thou our guard while troubles last,
And our eternal home!

Text: Based on Psalm 90(89), Isaac Watts, 1674–1748
Tune: ST. ANNE, C.M., attr. to William Croft, 1678–1727

1 O Lord, you died that all might live And rise to see the
2 Lord, bless our friend who died in you, As you have giv - en
3 In your green, pleas - ant pas - tures feed The sheep that you have
4 Di - rect us with your arm of might, That with our friend we

per - fect day. The full - ness of your mer - cy give To
him* re - lease. En - liv - en him* since he* was true, And
sum - moned hence; And by the still, cool wa - ters lead Your
may all come To dwell with - in your cit - y bright, Je -

REFRAIN

this our friend for whom we pray.
give him* ev - er - last - ing peace.   O Lamb of God, Re -
flock in lov - ing prov - i - dence.
ru - sa - lem, our heav'n - ly home.

deem - er blest, Grant him* e - ter - nal light and rest.

Alter gender of pronoun accordingly.

Text: Richard Frederick Littledale, 1833–1890
Tune: MELITA, L.M. with refrain, John Bacchus Dykes, 1823–1876

84 Peace Prayer

*Use D tuning

Words: John Foley, s.j., based on a prayer of St. Francis of Assisi
Music: John Foley, s.j., copyright ©1976, 1979, John Foley, s.j., and North American Liturgy Resources, 10802 North 23rd Avenue, Phoenix, Arizona 85029. All rights reserved. Used with permission.

85 Praise, My Soul, the King of Heaven

(Lower key at number 96C)

1 Praise, my soul, the King of heav - en;
2 Praise him for his grace and fa - vor
3 Fa - ther - like he tends and spares us,
4 An - gels, help us to a - dore him,

To his feet your trib - ute bring; Ran - somed,
To all peo - ple in dis - tress; Praise him
Well our fee - ble frame he knows; In his
You be - hold him face to face; Sun and

healed, re - stored, for - giv - en, Ev - er - more his
still the same as ev - er, Slow to chide and
hands he gen - tly bears us, Res - cues us from
moon, bow down be - fore him; Join the prais - es

prais - es sing: Al - le - lu - ia! Al - le -
swift to bless: *Praise him! Praise him! Praise him!
all our foes: *Praise him! Praise him! Praise him!
of our race:

*During Lent

150

lu - ia!   Glo - rious   in   his   faith - ful - ness.
Praise   him!   Wide - ly   yet   his   mer - cy   flows.
Praise   with   us   the   God   of   grace.

Praise the ev - er - last - ing King.

Text: Based on Psalm 103(102), Henry Francis Lyte, 1793–1847
Tune: LAUDA ANIMA 87.87.87, John Goss, 1800–1880

Jesus, Remember Me

Je - sus,   re - mem-ber me   when you come in - to your

King - dom.   Je - sus,   re - mem - ber me

when   you   come   in - to   your   King - dom.

Text: Luke 23:42
Tune: Jacques Berthier, copyright ©1978, 1980, 1981, Les Presses de Taize,
   with license to G.I.A. Publications, Inc. All rights reserved. Used with permission.

See What Goodness*
(Hymn Form, Alternate tune)

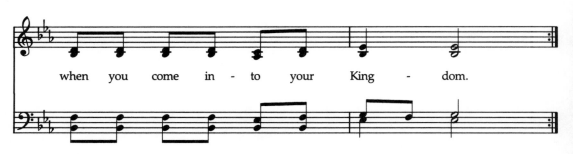

*The text as set below may be sung with this tune,
   or IN BABILONE (no. 87A), or other tunes of 87.87.D meter.

1 Blest be God, by whose great mercy
We are baptized in the Son.
Set apart as holy people,
We are God's and not our own.

Refrain:
See what goodness God has shown us,
From the reign of sin set free.
See how lavishly God loves us,
Making us a family.

2 We are made in God's own image;
On us is the Spirit poured.
We are cleansed in saving water;
We are clothed in Christ the Lord. *(Refrain)*

3 Rescued from the pow'r of darkness,
Brought into resplendent light,
Offer thanks for loving mercy,
Praise for gentleness and might! *(Refrain)*

Text: Delores Dufner, o.s.b., copyright ©1984, the Sisters of St. Benedict, St. Joseph, Minn. 56374
Tune: HYMN TO JOY, 87.87.D, adapted in 1846 by Edward Hodges,
    1796–1867, from Ludwig van Beethoven, 1770–1827

See What Goodness

(Hymn Form, Alternate tune)

Tune: IN BABILONE 87.87.D. Traditional Dutch melody found in
Oude en Nieuwe Hollantse Boerenliyies en Contradansen, c. 1710

88 I Heard the Voice of Jesus Say

1 I heard the voice of Je - sus say, "Come un - to me and
2 I heard the voice of Je - sus say, "Be - hold, I free - ly
3 I heard the voice of Je - sus say, "I am this dark world's

rest; And in your wear - i - ness lay down Your
give The liv - ing wa - ter, thirst - y one: Stoop
light; Look un - to me, your morn shall rise, And

head up - on my breast." I came to Je - sus
down and drink and live." I came to Je - sus
all your day be bright." I looked to Je - sus

as I was, So wear - y, worn, and sad; I
and I drank Of that life - giv - ing stream; My
and I found In him my star, my sun; and

found in   him   a   rest - ing place, And   he has made   me   glad.
thirst was quenched, my   soul re - vived, And now I   live   in   him.
in   that   light   of   life   I'll walk Till   all my days are   done.

Text: Horatius Bonar, 1808–1889
Tune: KINGSFOLD, harm. and arr. by Ralph Vaughan Williams, 1872–1958,
    setting from *The English Hymnal,* copyright ©Oxford University Press. Not for sale outside the U.S.A.

89

Stand Firm in Faith

1 Stand firm in faith, For gra - cious is the Lord.
2 Stand firm in faith, O friends who weep and mourn.
3 Stand firm in faith, For God calls us his friends.

Hold fast to hope; Our God will keep his Word.
Those who have died To new life have been born.
Hold fast to hope; His ten - der care he sends.

Grow strong in love; Your joy will be re - stored.
Splen - dor and grace Shall their fair souls a - dorn.
Grow strong in love; God's good - ness nev - er ends.

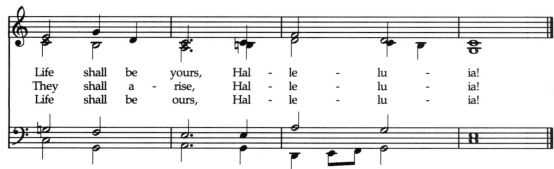

Life shall be yours, Hal - le - lu - ia!
They shall a - rise, Hal - le - lu - ia!
Life shall be ours, Hal - le - lu - ia!

Text: Delores Dufner, O.S.B., copyright ©1983, the Sisters of St. Benedict, St. Joseph, Minn. 56374
Tune: 46.46.46.44, copyright ©1983, Jay Hunstiger, 4545 Wichita Trail, Medina, Minn. 55340

(Higher key at number 72)

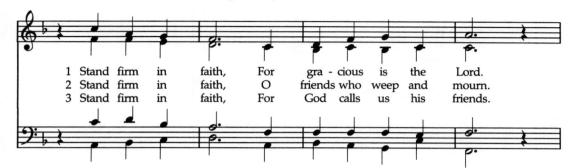

1 Stand firm in faith, For gra - cious is the Lord.
2 Stand firm in faith, O friends who weep and mourn.
3 Stand firm in faith, For God calls us his friends.

Hold fast to hope; Our God will keep his Word.
Those who have died To new life have been born.
Hold fast to hope; His ten - der care he sends.

Grow strong in love; Your joy will be re - stored.
Splen - dor and grace Shall their fair souls a - dorn.
Grow strong in love; God's good - ness nev - er ends.

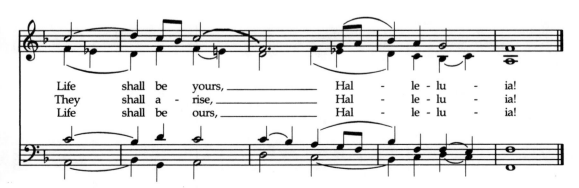

Life shall be yours, _____ Hal - le - lu - ia!
They shall a - rise, _____ Hal - le - lu - ia!
Life shall be ours, _____ Hal - le - lu - ia!

Tune: SINE NOMINE 10.10.10 with alleluias, Ralph Vaughan Williams, 1872–1958,
from the *English Hymnal*, copyright ©Oxford University Press

91 The Day of Resurrection

(Lower key at number 80B)

1 The day of res-ur-rec-tion! Earth, tell it out a-broad,
2 Let hearts be purged of e-vil That we may see a-right
3 Now let the heav'ns be joy-ful, Let earth its song be-gin,
4 Then praise we God the Fa-ther, And praise we Christ his Son,

The pass-o-ver of glad-ness The pass-o-ver of God.
The Lord in rays e-ter-nal Of res-ur-rec-tion light,
Let all the world keep tri-umph And all there is there-in.
With them the Ho-ly Spir-it E-ter-nal Three in One;

From death to life e-ter-nal, From sin's do-min-ion free,
And list-'ning to his ac-cents, May hear, so calm and plain,
Let all things, seen and un-seen, Their notes of glad-ness blend;
Till all the ran-somed num-ber Fall down be-fore the throne,

Our Christ has brought us o-ver With hymns of vic-to-ry.
His own "All hail!" and hear-ing, May raise the vic-tor strain.
For Christ the Lord has ris-en, Our joy that has no end!
And hon-or, pow'r, and glo-ry As-cribe to God a-lone!

Text: John of Damascus, c. 696–c. 754, tr. John M. Neale, 1818–1866, alt.
Tune: ELLACOMBE C.M.D., Württemberg Hymnal, 1784

Crown Him with Many Crowns

92

1 Crown him with man-y crowns, The Lamb up-on his throne;
2 Crown him the Lord of life, who tri-umphed o'er the grave,
3 Crown him the Lord of love, Be-hold his hands and side,
4 Crown him the Lord of years, The ris-en Lord sub-lime,

Hark! how the heaven-ly an-them drowns All mu-sic but its own.
and rose vic-to-rious in the strife For those he came to save.
Rich wounds yet vis-i-ble a-bove In beau-ty glo-ri-fied.
Cre-a-tor of the roll-ing spheres, The Mas-ter of all time.

A-wake, my soul, and sing Of him who set us free,
His glo-ries now we sing, Who died and rose on high,
No an-gel in the sky Can full-y bear that sight,
All hail, Re-deem-er, hail! For you have died for me;

And hail him as your heav'n-ly King Through all e-ter-ni-ty.
Who died, e-ter-nal life to bring, And lives that death may die.
But down-ward bends his burn-ing eye At mys-ter-ies so bright.
Your praise and glo-ry shall not fail Through-out e-ter-ni-ty.

Text: Based on Rev. 19:12; Matthew Bridges, 1800–1894
Tune: DIADEMATA S.M.D., George Job Elvey, 1816–1893

There's a Wideness in God's Mercy

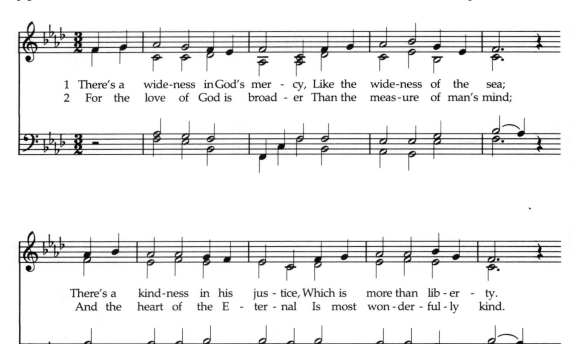

1 There's a wide-ness in God's mer - cy, Like the wide-ness of the sea;
2 For the love of God is broad - er Than the meas-ure of man's mind;

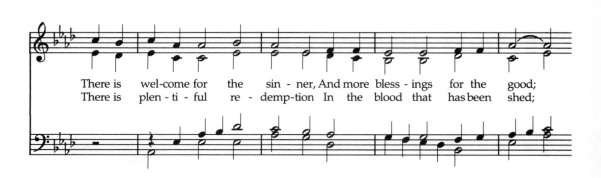

There's a kind-ness in his jus - tice, Which is more than lib - er - ty.
And the heart of the E - ter - nal Is most won-der - ful - ly kind.

There is wel-come for the sin - ner, And more bless - ings for the good;
There is plen - ti - ful re - demp-tion In the blood that has been shed;

There is mer - cy with the Sav - ior; There is heal - ing in his blood.
There is joy for all the mem - bers Now at one with Christ our Head.

Text: Frederick William Faber, 1814–1863, alt.
Tune: 87.87.D, Gerard Wojchowski, o.s.b., copyright ©1965, 1977, The Order of St. Benedict, Inc., Collegeville, Minn.

Till We See God's Face*

1 Wait when the seed is plant - ed, Wait for the rain to fall;
2 Hope when the sun is set - ting, Hope through the dark of night;
3 Trust in the new spring's prom - ise, Trust through the sum - mer's heat;

Wait for the rest - less green sprout, Wait while the plant grows tall.
Hope though the moon is wan - ing, Hope as we long for light.
Trust in the dy - ing au - tumn, Trust through the win - ter sleet.

Wait for the com - ing Sav - ior, Wait through the heart's slow race;
Hope for the com - ing Sav - ior, Hope through the heart's slow race;
Trust in the com - ing Sav - ior, Trust in the heart's slow race;

Wait for the king - dom's dawn - ing, Wait till we see God's face!
Hope for the king - dom's dawn - ing, Hope till we see God's face!
Trust in the king - dom's dawn - ing, Trust till we see God's face!

*This text may be sung to AURELIA (no. 94A) or other tunes of 76.76.D meter.

Text: Delores Dufner, o.s.b., copyright ©1983, the Sisters of St. Benedict, St. Joseph, Minn. 56374
Tune: GAUDETE, 76.76.D, copyright ©1983, Jay Hunstiger, 4545 Wichita Trail, Medina, Minn. 55340

94A

Till We See His Face

(Alternate tune)

(Lower key at number 80A)

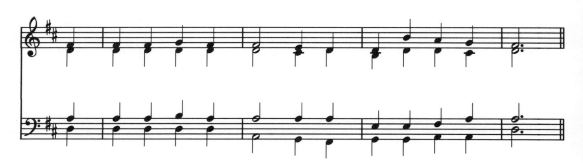

Tune: AURELIA 76.76.D, Samuel Sebastian Wesley, 1864

Love Is Come Again

1 Now the green blade ris - eth from the bur - ied grain,
2 In the grave they laid him, Love whom they had slain,
3 Forth he came at Eas - ter, like the ri - sen grain,

Wheat that in dark earth ma - ny days has lain;
Think - ing that nev - er he would wake a - gain,
He that for three days in the grave had lain.

Love lives a - gain, that with the dead has been;
Laid in the earth like grain that sleeps un - seen:
Quick from the dead my ri - sen Lord is seen:

Love is come a - gain, like wheat that spring - eth green.

Text: J.M.C. Crum, 1872–1958
Tune: NOEL NOUVELET, 11.11.10.10. harm. Martin Shaw, 1875–1958,
  from *The Oxford Book of Carols*, copyright ©Oxford University Press

Bless the Father
Alternate Tune

1 Bless the Father of our Savior, Praise him for his gracious love.
We are washed in living water; made new people in God's joy.
Here we celebrate his mercy. Let us pray and be renewed!

2 From the risen Christ's own promise, new birth draws its faithful life.
Guarded for us we inherit living hope that conquers death.
Gifts of grace for our salvation. Now rejoice and be refreshed.

3 From the water of salvation, we arise to promised life.
By the Spirit's pow'r unfading, looking toward the final age,
We await God's final Kingdom. Now give thanks; we are received.

Text: Rev. Michael Jones; for use in the public domain
Tune: REGENT SQUARE 87.87.87, Henry Smart, 1867

Bless the Father

(Alternate tune)

1 Bless the Father of our Savior, Praise him for his gracious love.
  We are washed in living water; made new people in God's joy.
  Here we celebrate his mercy. Let us pray and be renewed!

2 From the risen Christ's own promise, new birth draws its faithful life.
  Guarded for us we inherit living hope that conquers death.
  Gifts of grace for our salvation. Now rejoice and be refreshed.

3 From the water of salvation, we arise to promised life.
  By the Spirit's pow'r unfading, looking toward the final age,
  We await God's final Kingdom. Now give thanks; we are received.

Text: Rev. Michael Jones; for use in the public domain
Tune: ST. THOMAS (Webbe) 87.87.87, prob. by John Francis Wade, c. 1711-1786, in *Cantus Diversi*, 1751

96c
Bless the Father
(Alternate Tune)
(Higher key at number 85)

1 Bless the Father of our Savior, Praise him for his gracious love.
  We are washed in living water; made new people in God's joy.
  Here we celebrate his mercy. Let us pray and be renewed!

2 From the risen Christ's own promise, new birth draws its faithful life.
  Guarded for us we inherit living hope that conquers death.
  Gifts of grace for our salvation. Now rejoice and be refreshed.

3 From the water of salvation, we arise to promised life.
  By the Spirit's pow'r unfading, looking toward the final age,
  We await God's final Kingdom. Now give thanks; we are received.

Text: Michael Jones; for use in the public domain
Tune: LAUDA ANIMA 87.87.87, John Goss, 1869

To Jesus Christ, Our Sovereign King

1 To Je - sus Christ, our sov - 'reign King, Who is the world's sal - va - tion, All
2 Your reign ex - tend, O King be - nign, To ev - 'ry land and na - tion; For
3 To you and to your Church, great King, We pledge our hearts' ob - la - tion Un -

praise and hom - age do we bring And thanks and ad - o - ra - tion.
in your king - dom, Lord di - vine, A - lone we find sal - va - tion.
til be - fore your throne we sing In end - less ju - bi - la - tion.

REFRAIN

Christ Je - sus, Vic - tor! Christ Je - sus, Rul - er!

Christ Je - sus, Lord and Re - deem - er!

Text: Margin B. Hellriegel, 1890–1981, alt. Used with permission of Irene C. Mueller. Copyright transferred 1978.
Tune: ICH GLAUB' AN GOTT 87.87. with refrain, *Gesangbuch*, Mainz, 1900, alt.

98 We Know That Christ Is Raised

1 We know that Christ is raised and dies no more. _____
2 We share by wa - ter in his sav - ing death. _____
3 The Fa - ther's splen - dor clothes the Son with life. _____
4 A new cre - a - tion comes to life and grows. _____

Em - braced by death, he broke its fear - ful hold, _____
Re - born, we share with him an Eas - ter life, _____
The Spir - it's fis - sion shakes the Church of God. _____
As Christ's new bod - y takes on flesh and blood. _____

And our de - spair he turned to blaz - ing joy.
As liv - ing mem - bers of our Sav - ior Christ.
Bap - tized, we live with God the Three in One.
The u - ni - verse re - stored and whole will sing:

[1-3]   [Final Ending]

Hal - le - lu - jah!   Hal - le - lu - jah!

Text: Copyright ©John B. Geyer, b. 1932, alt.
Tune: ENGELBERG 10.10.10.4, Charles V. Stanford, 1852–1924

170

When from Bondage

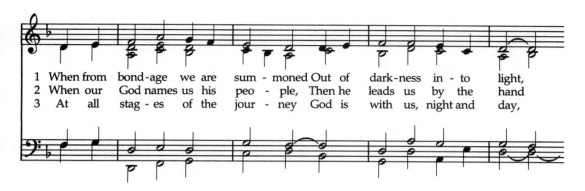

1 When from bond-age we are sum-moned Out of dark-ness in-to light,
2 When our God names us his peo-ple, Then he leads us by the hand
3 At all stag-es of the jour-ney God is with us, night and day,

We must go in hope and pa-tience, Walk by faith and not by sight.
Through a lone-ly bar-ren des-ert, To a great and glo-rious land.
With com-pas-sion for our weak-ness Ev-'ry step a-long the way.

Let us throw off all that hin-ders; Let us run the race to win!

Let us has-ten to our home-land And, re-joic-ing, en-ter in.

Text: Delores Dufner, o.s.b., copyright ©1984, the Sisters of St. Benedict, St. Joseph, Minn. 56374
Tune: 87.87.D, copyright ©1984, Jay Hunstiger, 4545 Wichita Trail, Medina, Minn. 55340

When from Bondage

(Alternate Tune)

Tune: AUSTRIA (HAYDN) 87.87.D, Franz Joseph Haydn, 1797

When from Bondage

(Alternate tune)

(Higher key at number 70B)

99B

Tune: PLEADING SAVIOR 87.87.D, *Plymouth Collection*, New York, 1855

100 The King of Love My Shepherd Is

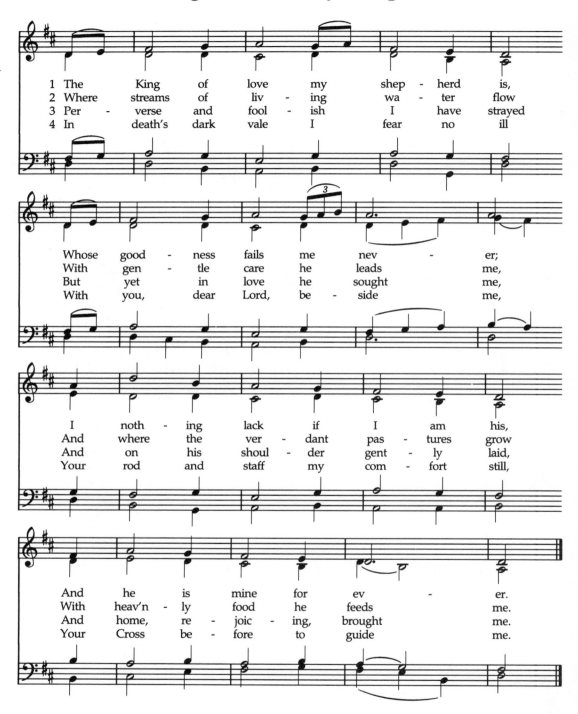

1 The King of love my shep - herd is,
2 Where streams of liv - ing wa - ter flow
3 Per - verse and fool - ish I have strayed
4 In death's dark vale I fear no ill

Whose good - ness fails me nev - er;
With gen - tle care he leads me,
But yet in love he sought me,
With you, dear Lord, be - side me,

I noth - ing lack if I am his,
And where the ver - dant pas - tures grow
And on his shoul - der gent - ly laid,
Your rod and staff my com - fort still,

And he is mine for ev - er.
With heav'n - ly food he feeds me.
And home, re - joic - ing, brought me.
Your Cross be - fore to guide me.

5 You spread a table in my sight,
Your saving grace bestowing;
And O what joy and true delight
From your pure chalice flowing!

6 And so through all the length of days
Your goodness fails me never;
Good Shepherd, may I sing your praise
Within your house for ever.

Text: Based on Ps. 22, Matt. 18, and Jn. 10, Sir Henry Williams Baker, 1821–1877
Tune: ST. COLUMBA (ERIN) 87.87, trad. Irish hymn melody. Acc. by Russell Woollen, 1980, copyright ©1980, ICEL

174

101

Let the Hungry Come to Me

1 Let the hun-gry come to Me, Let the poor be fed.
2 I my-self am liv-ing bread; Feed on Me and live.
3 Here a-mong you shall I dwell, Mak-ing all things new.
4 Nour-ished by the Word of God, Now we eat the Bread.

Let the thirs-ty come and drink, Share My wine and bread.
In this cup, My blood for you; Drink the wine I give.
You shall be my ve-ry own, I, your God-with-you.
With the gift of God's own life, Hun-gry hearts are fed.

Though you have no mon-ey, Come to Me and eat.
All who eat My bod-y, All who drink My blood
Blest are you in-vi-ted, To my wed-ding feast.
Man-na in the des-ert, In our dark-est night!

Drink the cup I of-fer; Feed on fin-est wheat!
Shall have joy for-ev-er, Share the life of God.
You shall live for-ev-er, All your joys in-creased.
Food for pil-grim peo-ple, Pledge of glo-ry bright!

5 Many grains become one loaf,
   Many grapes, the wine.
   So shall we one body be,
   Who together dine.
   As the bread is broken,
   As the wine is shared:
   So must we be given,
   Caring as Christ cared.

6 Risen Savior, walk with us,
   Lead us by the hand.
   Heal our blinded eyes and hearts,
   Help us understand.
   Lord, make known your presence
   At this table blest.
   Stay with us forever,
   God, our host and guest!

Text: Delores Dufner, o.s.b., copyright ©1983, the Sisters of St. Benedict, St. Joseph, Minn. 56374
Tune: ADORO TE 75.75.65.65., plainchant, mode V. Acc. by Irwin Udulutsch, o.f.m. cap.,
   copyright ©1959, 1977, The Order of St. Benedict, Inc.

102

Amazing Grace
(Lower key at number 103B)

1 A - maz - ing grace! How sweet the sound,
2 'Twas grace that taught my heart to fear,
3 The Lord has prom - ised good to me,
4 Through man - y dan - gers, toils, and snares,

That saved and strength - ened me!
And grace my fears re - lieved;
His word my hope se - cures
I have al - read - y come;

I once was lost, but now am found,
How pre - cious did that grace ap - pear
He will my shield and por - tion be
'Tis grace hath brought me safe thus far,

Was blind, but now I see.
The hour I first be - lieved!
As long as life en - dures.
And grace will lead me home.

Text: John Newton, 1725–1807
Tune: AMAZING GRACE, C.M. Early American melody, arr. by Edwin Othello Excell, 1851–1921.

I Call You to My Father's House

103

1. I call you to my Fa - ther's house, A
2. Lay down your sor - row, calm your fear; The
3. Al - though the way be hard and long In -
4. I have pre - pared a wed - ding feast Of
5. I call you to my Fa - ther's house, A

love - ly dwell - ing place. He comes to meet you
Fa - ther bids you come. With o - pen arms He
to the prom - ised land, Be not a - fraid to
fin - est food and wine. O join us at this
love - ly dwell - ing place. Be not a - fraid to

on the road, Arms read - y to em - brace.
wel - comes you To your e - ter - nal home.
walk with Me: I hold you by the hand.
ban - quet where My friends, the saints, now dine.
trav - el there And meet Him face to face.

Text: Delores Dufner, o.s.b., copyright © 1983, the Sisters of St. Benedict, St. Joseph, Minn., 56374
Tune: 87.87, copyright ©1983, Jay Hunstiger, 4545 Wichita Trail, Medina, Minn. 55340

103A   I Call You to My Father's House
(Alternate tune)
(Higher key at number 73)

Tune: LAND OF REST, C.M., trad. American melody, acc. by Sister Theophane Hytrek, o.s.f., copyright ©1980, ICEL

103B   I Call You to My Father's House
(Alternate Tune)
(Higher key at number 102)

Tune: AMAZING GRACE, C.M., early American melody, arr. by Edwin Othello Excell, 1851–1921

Lord of All Hopefulness

104

1 Lord of all hope - ful - ness, Lord of all joy,
2 Lord of all ea - ger - ness, Lord of all faith,
3 Lord of all kind - li - ness, Lord of all grace,
4 Lord of all gen - tle - ness, Lord of all calm,

Whose trust, ev - er child - like no cares could de - stroy:
Whose strong hands were skilled at the plane and the lathe:
Your hands swift to wel - come, your arms to em - brace:
Whose voice is con - tent - ment, whose pres - ence is balm:

Be there at our wak - ing, and give us, we pray,
Be there at our la - bors, and give us, we pray,
Be there at our hom - ing, and give us, we pray,
Be there at our sleep - ing, and give us, we pray,

Your bliss in our hearts, Lord, at the break of the day.
Your strength in our hearts, Lord, at the noon of the day.
Your love in our hearts, Lord, at the eve of the day.
Your peace in our hearts, Lord, at the end of the day.

Text: Jan Struther, 1901–1953, copyright ©Oxford University Press
Tune: SLANE 10.11.11.12, Irish ballad melody; adap. The Church Hymnary, 1927, harm. copyright ©1985, *The Hymnal 1982*

The Strife Is O'er

REFRAIN

Al - le - lu - ia! Al - le - lu - ia! Al - le - lu - ia!

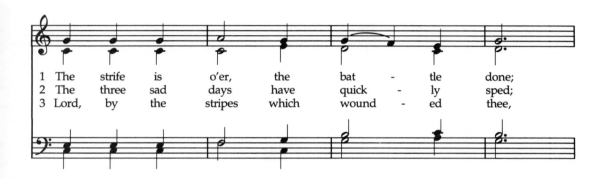

1 The strife is o'er, the bat - tle done;
2 The three sad days have quick - ly sped;
3 Lord, by the stripes which wound - ed thee,

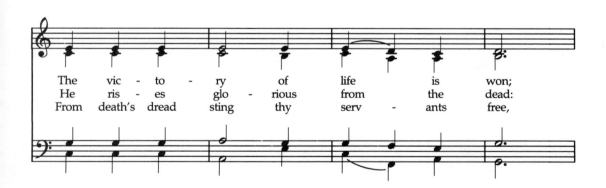

The vic - to - ry of life is won;
He ris - es glo - rious from the dead:
From death's dread sting thy serv - ants free,

(to refrain)

The song of tri - umph has be - gun. Al - le - lu - ia!
All glo - ry to our ris - en Head! Al - le - lu - ia!
That we may live and sing to thee: Al - le - lu - ia!

Text: *Finita iam sunt praelia*, tr. by Francis Pott, 1832–1909, alt.
Tune: VICTORY 888 with alleluias, Giovanni Pierluigi da Palestrina, c. 1525–1594

What Wondrous Love Is This

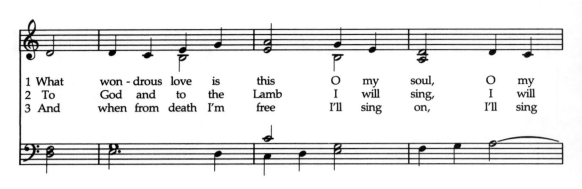

1 What won - drous love is this O my soul, O my
2 To God and to the Lamb I will sing, I will
3 And when from death I'm free I'll sing on, I'll sing

soul? What won - drous love is this O my
sing; To God and to the Lamb I will
on; And when from death I'm free, I'll sing

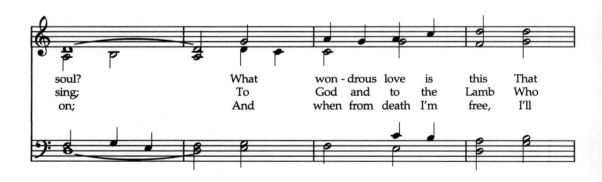

soul? What won - drous love is this That
sing; To God and to the Lamb Who
on; And when from death I'm free, I'll

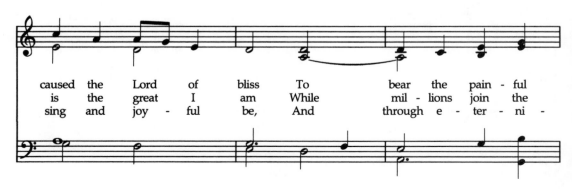

caused the Lord of bliss To bear the pain - ful
is the great I am While mil - lions join the
sing and joy - ful be, And through e - ter - ni -

cross   for   my   soul,   for   my   soul;   To
theme,   I   will   sing,   I   will   sing;   While
ty   I'll   sing   on,   I'll   sing   on!   And

bear   the   pain - ful   cross   for   my   soul? _____
mil - lions   join   the   theme,   I   will   sing. _____
through e - ter - ni - ty,   I'll   sing   on. _____

Text: Rev. Alexander Means, 1835, alt.
Tune: WONDROUS LOVE 66.63.66.66.63, William Walker's *Southern Harmony*, 1835.
   Acc. by Sister Theophane Hytrek, o.s.f., 1980, copyright ©1980, ICEL

Christ the Lord Is Ris'n Today

1 Christ, the Lord, is ris'n to - day; Chris-tians, haste your vows to pay;
2 Christ, the vic - tim un - de - filed, God and sin - ners rec - on - ciled;
3 Say, O wond'ring Mar - y say What you saw a - long the way.
4 Christ, who once for sin - ners bled, Now the first - born from the dead,

Of - fer now your prais - es meet At the Pas - chal Vic - tim's feet.
When in strange and aw - ful strife, Met to - geth - er death and life.
"I be - held, where Christ had lain, Emp - ty tomb and an - gels twain;
Throned in end - less might and pow'r, Lives and reigns for ev - er - more.

For the sheep the Lamb has bled, Sin - less in the sin - ner's stead.
Chris-tians, on this hap - py day, Haste with joy your vows to pay.
I be - held the glo - ry bright Of the ris - ing Lord of light.
Hail e - ter - nal hope on high! Hail, our King of vic - to - ry!

Christ, the Lord, is ris'n on high; Now he lives, no more to die.
Christ, the Lord, is ris'n on high; Now he lives, no more to die.
Christ, my hope, is ris'n a - gain; Now he lives, and lives to reign."
Hail, our Prince of life a - dored! Help and save us, gra-cious Lord!

Text: *Victimae Paschali Laudes*, attr. to Wipo of Burgundy, 10th cent.
Tune: VICTIMAE PASCHALI 77.77.D, *Katholisches Gesangbuch*, 1859

The Head That Once Was Crowned

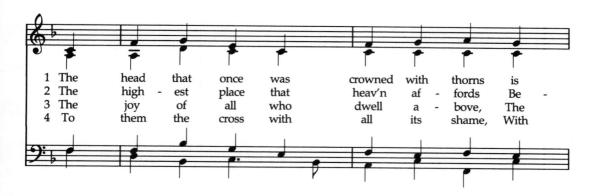

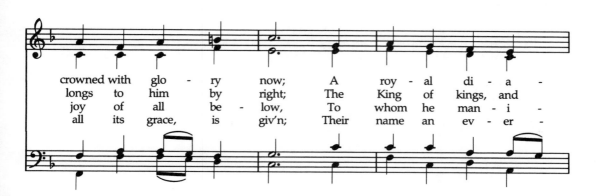

5 They suffer with their Lord below;
They reign with him above;
Their profit and their joy to know
The myst'ry of his love.

6 The cross he bore is life and health,
Though shame and death to him,
His people's hope, his people's wealth,
Their everlasting theme.

Text: Based on Hebrews 2:9–10, Thomas Kelly, 1769–1855
Tune: ST. MAGNUS, C.M., attr. to Jeremiah Clark, c. 1670–1707

INDEX OF TITLES